Metap[illegible] f th[illegible]

A Philosophical Analysis of Iron Maiden

Volume I
1980-1984

Jerome Reuter

St Rooster Books 2024

Praise for Jerome Reuter's previous work...

Through the Mist and the Madness: An Analytical Thesis on the First Three Metallica Albums

"Jerome Reuter and St. Rooster Press present here a thoroughly entertaining and highly readable analysis of the first three Metallica albums...While the focus of this review is on the lyrical content, Jerome also skillfully adds vital context to the times in which these albums were released, comparing and contrasting the approach of the band to their peers and other cultural events of the mid 1980's. The writing itself I must compliment for its conversational tone, never coming across as too academic or stuffy...I wholeheartedly and strongly recommend this book to fans of Metallica, or fans of very well-written and researched music analysis!" **-Mathew Henshaw**

Electric Funeral: Black Sabbath and the Cultural Landscape 1970-1975

"This book is absolutely fascinating as well as educational. The author has taken on a substantial research project and put out into the world a thoughtful and intellectual look at how world events and the alchemy of the band members themselves created Black Sabbath. Yes, they were a head-banging, proto-metal band, but the author shows us just how much more they were than just that. This is a great book that's quite a bit different from other looks at Black Sabbath and/or the birth of metal." **-Amazon reader**

Metaphysics of the Beast: A Philosophical Analysis of Iron Maiden

Volume I
1980-1984

By
Jerome Reuter

St Rooster Books 2024

First edition

Contact St Rooster Book at
Holyrooster76 @ gmail . com

Contents

A Letter from Purgatory and a Declaration of Intent from the Author

If you're reading this, congratulations, you've taken the first steps with me on a journey into the realms of theory and philosophy. Our final destination is where they merge with criticism and subjective thought. The complexity of the subject matter that I've chosen is such that it's virtually impossible to use simple terminology to describe it in detail. Therefore, I plan on going far beyond basic critique. The challenge that presents itself in any form of discourse is remaining objective with the material that's being dissected. In an age where the lives of artists are judged on the same level as their creative output, separating sincerity from the phonies who worry themselves with such details becomes an even greater challenge. Terms such as "problematic" have become commonplace, as is the introductory phrase "we need to talk about…."

The book you hold in your hands will not be hampered by such meager and pedestrian terminologies. Instead, I offer you a journey into a reality that's completely divorced from our own. One that encompasses the microcosm and macrocosm and delves into the recorded material of one of the greatest bands to ever exist–Iron Maiden.

To say they've had a meaningful impact on me would be quite an understatement. Hearing "Flight of Icarus" on the radio for the first time as an impressionable pre-teen and acquiring the audio cassette of *Live After Death* would forever shift the paradigm of my personal taste, but I digress. While this book is about Iron Maiden, I do not intend to follow the traditional discourse patterns that music journalists often accompany. Nor will I recount the historical facts of their formative years in London and the unwavering dedication of its founder, Steve Harris. These tasks have been performed many times before by authors who are much more qualified than me. Most notably by Geoff Barton and Mick Wall. So, what will I be offering?

In my book about the first three Metallica albums, I took a deep dive into the recorded material and the various changes happening at a pivotal point in the genre, of which the music of Iron Maiden was pivotal. When I shifted gears to discuss Black Sabbath, I focused on the tumultuous events of the time period and the shifts in popular culture that helped formulate the world in which the Sabbath existed. The manufactured reality created by art and the physical one in which we exist continuously intermingle with one another, and it's this union that I've dedicated a considerable amount of time writing about. As the writing process is very much non-linear, I have no intention of repeating previous formulas. The approach I've decided to take is different, and I hope your journey with me will be enlightening.

In the book you hold before you, we will deal with the aspects of the microcosm and macrocosm. The latter of these two will be Iron Maiden themselves, and the former will be the recorded material. There is a Sadeian approach that I plan to undertake. In *The 120 Days of Sodom,* the libertines represent physical manifestations of law, religion, and government institutions. This reality is confined to Silling, the story's location, and the reality within the book's pages in the Bastille, where the Marquis de Sade constructed his "most impure tale ever written." As for what you're about to read, each album will exist in its own reality, divorced from meaningless trivia and the diatribes that typically exist within the realm of common discourse.

Like the Marquis de Sade, I ask that you come with me, a friendly reader, and prepare yourself, for we're about to enter a world of philosophy and metaphysics. A world in which all art is subjective, and the offerings of Iron Maiden will be held in the same regard as the writings of Socrates and de Sade. And much like the Socratic method of philosophical thought, all things will be subjective.

I want nothing more than to question with introspection and curiosity what each song represents. All thoughts and assumptions shall be challenged and questioned to their fullest potential, and there's no limitation to how deep we shall dive. As Roman emperor and philosopher Marcus Aurelias stated in his book *Meditations,* "Look inward; don't let the true nature or value of anything elude you." Looking inward is what I strive to do with this text.

Up the Irons!

Jerome Reuter, 2023

Iron Maiden (1980): The Formative Years of the Neophyte

If this were normal discourse regarding the recorded history of Iron Maiden, it might be easy to assume that we would begin with their formative years in the East End of London. Perhaps we would discuss the background and upbringing of the individuals involved. We might even establish the process that led to the group's demo, *The Soundhouse Tapes*. I could certainly recount the tireless efforts of founding member Steve Harris to get a solid lineup in place, which itself involved the bassist going through an almost endless amount of lineup changes, all the while remaining steadfast and determined to accomplish his goal. Because I hope to offer a different approach that deviates from common expectations, I find it more beneficial to begin with the group's self-titled full-length, which arrived in 1980. And while we won't be diving into the facets and behind-the-scenes drama that so many other books might gravitate towards, we will be mentioning the various players involved in each release and how they helped catapult Iron Maiden's sound into the stratosphere of sonic perfection. The players at this stage included the twin guitar team of Dave Murray and Dennis Stratton, drummer Clive Burr, and Paul Di'Anno on vocals. Of course, behind it all, composing, leading, and never once compromising his artistic vision, was founding member Steve Harris on bass.

It's worth noting that human beings are products of their environment. This is basic psychology, and there's no question that many different forms of art have come into existence because of the surroundings in which their creators inhabit. In the case of Iron Maiden, their early works are very much products of the East End of London. Remarkably, this location has always shared a very interesting relationship with popular culture, one that's not always flattering. The manufactured reality that's been constructed on stage and in film has certainly had fun with cockney accents, some of which have been greatly exaggerated and depicted in a world of poverty and dim-wittedness. Whether it's Burt the Chimney Sweep from *Mary Poppins,* portrayed by Dick Van Dyke in one of the most unconvincing roles ever put to celluloid, Audrey Hepburn's role of Eliza Doolittle in *My Fair Lady,* which also starred Stanley Holloway as her cockney and comical father, there's always been tongue-in-cheek humor at the expense of the location. With phrases such as "Guv'nah" repeated in an over-the-top characterization of the residents.

While many have certainly had their fun laughing at the differences in social class, the reality of the East End has been less comical and more dreary, dark, and, at times macabre. The Victorian era of England is sometimes thought of as a posh and sophisticated world where nannies and governesses tend to children, and afternoon tea takes precedence over important matters of the day. The reality of life in the East End during this unique time period was one of degradation, poverty, and desperation for an escape of some sort. This isn't at all the fault of the people who inhabited the area, as the Industrial Revolution of the 1800s brought about pollution and overcrowding. Throughout this leap forward in industrial progress and production, slums inhabited by an increased population density could be found all over Europe and the United States.

Perhaps the East End might not have become as infamous in the public consciousness had it not been for a section of the city known as Whitechapel. It was in this area in 1888 that the murders of five sex workers occurred. These crimes, still unsolved to this day, are linked to a mysterious and unknown serial murderer known as Jack the Ripper. The Ripper murders, known for their unrestrained barbarity and the sensationalized coverage in the English press, remain a source of macabre fascination for historians, true crime buffs, and even ghost hunters who claim that the spirit of Elizabeth "Long Liz" Stride still frequents the area. The photographs of Catherine Eddowes and Mary Jane Kelley disemboweled and mutilated certainly sparked the morbid fascination with sociopathy and violent crime that we still see in our modern era. The violence begat from poverty certainly plays a role in much of the material that will take shape on the first two Iron Maiden albums.

As we've seen through the films of such directors as Pier Paolo Pasolini and Roman Polanski, the cruel hardships of poverty generate an honest art that's born out of desperation and decay. To list every artist to whom this applies to would be an arduous task in itself and one that would greatly detract from the discourse that I'm attempting to offer. Safe to say, the grit and determination of the band and the power of the music that would emanate from their albums throughout the years contain a form of escapism that stretches out far beyond the squalid streets of London's dangerous neighborhoods.

The urban hardships and blight don't just manifest themselves in the environment that spawned Iron Maiden as a band; they also find their way onto the cover art of the album. This certainly establishes a direct continuity with both the band's environment and their artistic expression. The reality that I alluded to earlier can best be personified by a fictional character who has become just as recognizable as the music of the band themselves–their iconic mascot, Eddie. The conceptual artwork of Derek Riggs sees the mascot changing between each album cover and certainly embodies the band's ability to adapt and evolve over time. Like Iron Maiden themselves, never complacent with one distinguishable form. And it's the cover of the debut album that immediately sets the tone for what we're going to experience. Eddie stands against a brick wall with the dark alleys of the east end behind him, illuminated slightly by isolated lampposts; this image depicts the darkness and desolation with brief moments of respite. A red window in the backdrop will be central to one of the songs on the album and itself be the first installment of a self-contained mythology that will span across four different albums. Eddie, the mascot, could possibly represent the emergence of the new subculture that was beginning to take form amid the further emergence of the NWOBHM (New Wave of British Heavy Metal.). The outsider exists within a city inhabited by thousands who fail to understand him and don't even bother to attempt to. If the artwork establishes the bleak world of the East End, then the album's opening track reinforces the dangers of the area in question.

Prowler

This world of danger and uncertainty for those who call the East End, or any highly populated urban area home is established on the album's opening track, "Prowler." To someone unfamiliar with the darker aspects of London's history, "Prowler" might come across as a song about a flasher, all too eager to show off his manhood to some of the female citizens who populate the same area. However, knowing what we know now about Jack the Ripper and some of the more violent crimes that plagued England throughout the 20th century, we can be led to believe that "Prowler" is about the serial murderer stalking his victims and partaking in self-inflicted sexual gratification. "Prowler" relies on a first-person narrative, placing the listener into the mindset of a perpetrator and normalizing the deviant behavior as another fact of life in the area in question. It certainly plays to the morbid fascination with behavior that deviates from normalcy. The fact that events such as these are a regular occurrence illustrates an image of an environment that spawned such a bold new art form.

"Walking through the city, looking oh so pretty" hints at a level of voyeurism and desire that has been a common trait in many serial murderers throughout history. Lyrical passages such as "I've just got to find my way" and "got me talking, but nothing's with me" can be interpreted as the balance between madness and brief moments of sanity in which the narrator exists. The narrator attempts to "find his way" and, at the same time, has an internal dialogue, possibly with voices or psychopathic delusion. "See the ladies flashing, all their legs and lashes" is tantamount to the delusion in which the narrator feels tempted by others. This is a common aspect found in many perpetrators who feel as if they're being "led on" by their victims.

The one lyrical passage that hints at the perpetrator flashing is "See me crawling through the bushes with it wide open…can you believe it? It's the real thing, girl." "The real thing" is an obvious method of describing the narrator's manhood and hints at his internal ego that it's something coveted by others. Still, the reality of another woman in the East End becoming just another statistic in the never-ending tally of victims of violent crime is evident in the song. "Prowler" is a genuine product of the East End and the violent behavior of the criminal mind that thrives in overpopulated and poverty-stricken areas. It's an unflinching look at life within the confines of the inner city. The lyrical content could easily be described as ambiguous. A fictional narrative closely based on reality, this is an expose of what all too many people end up facing at one time or another.

Remember Tomorrow

Earlier, we established the band's mascot, Eddie, and how his continuous transformation on each album demonstrates the evolution and progression of the band and their refusal to remain complacent in the pursuit of perfection. Like the act of writing itself, the material on each album is very much a nonlinear exercise. "Remember Tomorrow," considering its placement in between "Prowler" and "Running Free" on the album, certainly illustrates this concept. And, just like I've set out to do with the discourse I'm presenting, the song is more in line with metaphysics and has quite a few interpretations that are open to conjecture.

Like any ritual, that is, an event that is meant to alter reality, Remember Tomorrow permeates with the type of atmosphere that conjures up thoughts of the esoteric and a higher plane of consciousness. A slight departure from the world in which we were just engulfed, "Remember Tomorrow's" lyrical themes are otherworldly. This certainly alludes to the need for escapism from the confines of poverty that were prominent within the East End. "Unchain the colors before my eyes. Yesterday's Sorrows, tomorrow's white lies" is a lyrical passage that requires a bit of exploration on my part.

"Unchain the colors before my eyes" hints at the illusion of the physical world and its bright colors and appearance. These can be interpreted as the flickering images of a TV screen, being nothing more than a prison that shackles the narrator to what society places before him. "Yesterday's sorrows, tomorrow's white lies" speaks to the enlightenment of sorts, with the trouble and worries of the past becoming nothing more than falsehoods and delusions in the future. A child grows up with expectations and a certain perspective that dissipates with growth. Almost anyone can relate to the realization that what we thought the world was at one point is very different from the reality that exists.

"Tears for remembrance, and tears for joy. Tears for somebody and this lonely boy" can be interpreted as the melancholy that happens during the process of spiritual inertia. That is to say, all moments and events are nothing more than sorrow and the onward droning of existence. "Out in the madness, the all-seeing eye" might possibly allude to the eye of Sauron from J.R. Tolkien, or it can possibly refer to a path of enlightenment or spiritual awakening that can be found somewhere, despite the physical world and its confinement. "Flickers above us, to light up the sky" furthers this conjecture, with it taking the form of a literal light to guide us through the trappings of existence. "Scan the horizons" is something that further describes this never-ending search. As much as I want to limit any comparisons to other notable works from other groups, I can't help but be reminded of Planet Caravan by Black Sabbath. Both songs describe the search for something more among the monotony of one's own environment.

Running Free

While there's certainly a considerable amount of content that one can unpack with "Remember Tomorrow," "Running Free" contains little in the way of pretense as to its intention regarding the subject matter. One in a long line of songs that champion the nomads operating outside the confines of the law, "Running Free" represents the popular image of the rebel, a la James Dean in *Rebel Without a Cause*. At the same time, the lyrical content depicts the individual, or in this case, a band, following a path toward their own destiny. If we stop for a moment and consider the drive and purpose that were fueling the band at this point in their career, the narrative of "Running Free" can be seen as the desire to follow the path less traveled, as Robert Frost might have put it. The existence of songs that champion "life on the road" is certainly nothing new, and many artists have used this structure to compare the following of a dream or desire with the outlaw who lives life on the edge and defines conformity.

The cover art for the single certainly reinforces this concept as a denim-clad individual shuffles down an alleyway. While Eddie has usually been front and center for many of the artistic offerings, he stands in the background, looking at the subject heading toward a future of uncertainty. Forgoing societal obligations and following the path of the individual in the sense of gratification and enlightenment has been a major part of many philosophical works since the days of Athenian orators. Eddie appears in the context of an omnipotent and transcendental force gazing upon the unknown character, looking after him in his journey towards ascension.

Lyrically, "Running Free" has the sort of depictions that accompany the anti-hero from stories that our sense of adventure and excitement gravitate toward. "Just 16, a pickup truck, out of money, out of luck. I've got no place to call my own, hit and gas, and here I go." Is a familiar narrative that many of us are familiar with. As previously stated, this repurposing to suit the band's ambition is certainly impressive but not unique. If it were projected in the manufactured reality of the film, a critical analysis might see it as subversion and social commentary. This classic narrative style is reinforced by the lyrical passages about how the narrator "spent the night at an L.A. jail." And while London and Los Angeles are just about as far apart as one can fathom, the idea of isolation and the pursuit of a lofty ambition is certainly a universal experience.

Phantom of the Opera

To properly define the purpose of art and philosophy is a virtually impossible task. Both are subjective and offer a variety of uses for a wide range of different purposes. Art serves in a two-fold method. At its best, it's completely selfish and owes nothing to the people who engage with it. Art is also the ultimate form of escapism, allowing us to enter a reality that's completely divorced from our own. Philosophy allows for discourse and explanation of both the physical and spiritual world that we exist within. It provides the ability to look at things beyond their face value and understand that there's more between the world that we see and what truly exists. When combined, art and philosophy allow us to take a detailed look at various forms of escapism and journey into the unknown and better understand them. In applying the Socratic method, we can hold all things in a subjective form.

This aspect is certainly present in "Phantom of the Opera." Known to a great many people as a popular Broadway musical and a multitude of film adaptations, including one where Lon Chaney portrayed the titular character, The Phantom has transcended the character first brought to life by French author Gaston Laroux in 1911. Throughout the years, he has become just as recognizable as Dracula or Frankenstein's Monster as a figure in the rich pantheon of gothic horror. He's become a romanticized figure in a realm of fantasy that allows for grandiose escapism.

If I were to offer my personal interpretation of what the *Phantom of the Opera* represents, it would be the act of invisible manipulation that musicians and other artists possess and weave upon their audiences. It's a ritualistic practice that has quite a lot in common with the magician at his altar. They both intend to alter the course of reality through their respective crafts. The Phantom's alter is the opera house in which he resides; the reality he alters is accomplished through the music in which he performs. As for the song of the same name, it's easily one of the most powerful and engrossing compositions that Iron Maiden has ever recorded, one which certainly encompasses the same intent from both the magician and the phantom respectively.

A composition that weaves in and out of multiple time changes and demonstrates the bands' ever-growing ability to build atmosphere with their music, the lyrical content elevates the song as we find ourselves within a Paris opera house, the events of Laroux's novel, involving both the Phantom and the protagonist of the story, Christine, unfolding before us. While obsession is usually associated with the Phantom, the lyrical content of the song also manages to encapsulate Christine's attraction to the mysterious entity vividly. The first verse seems to hint at a conversation between the Phantom and Christine and reinforces the awe and mystery that exists between the two of them. "I've been looking so long for you now, you won't get away from my grasp," and the preceding line of "You've been living so long in hiding, in hiding behind that false mask" almost takes the form of a duet between the antagonist and protagonist of the story. "You're standing in the wings waiting for the curtain to fall" places us within the location, viewing the Phantom's plans as they slowly begin to unfurl. In keeping with the tradition of the story, the song manages to weave its own spell of musical complexity that itself takes on an overtly operatic tone. While the lyrical content is typically where we would expect the story to unfold in its entirety, the musical composition is just as essential in placing us within the narrative.

In the song's third verse, we're issued a warning from another character from the novel, Raoul, to Christine. "Keep your distance; walk away. don't take his bait…watch your step; he's out to get you." Illustrates the danger that the Phantom thoroughly represents. The fourth and final verse returns to the form of a duet between Christine and the Phantom. "I'm running and hiding. In my dreams, you're always there" contrasts almost too perfectly with the following lyrical passage of "You're the phantom of the opera. You're the devil; you're just out to scare." Paints the imagery of these two characters expressing their feelings of obsession and repulsion. We're granted a perspective of voyeurism, and much like the source material, the song manages to exhibit a strong sense of erotic tension without being overly expressive.

Transylvania

Because the discourse I'm offering centers heavily upon philosophy, analyzing an instrumental might present itself as somewhat of a challenge. But, as the concluding number for the first side of the LP, "Transylvania" comes across as a manifestation of the fears that are found within the pages of gothic horror. Its placement on the album, which follows the conclusion of "Phantom of the Opera," is almost too fitting considering the song's subject material. And there's something to it that's authentically British. Transylvania, the land where shadows and folklore exist and superstition is taken as fact, certainly has a rich tradition with English horror, as the setting became romanticized in a variety of films from Hammer studios. The many films in which Christopher Lee portrayed

Dracula certainly brought the character to life to an entirely new generation of devotees. The British horror tradition of the graveyards, the moors, the woman in black, and the specters that haunt the countryside are all integral to the world of Hammer horror.

Its marching feeling and powerful mood allow the superstitions and folklore that are commonly associated with the faraway land to come to life in the mind's eye. The long and perilous journey that Harker takes to reach the forbidding fortress of Count Dracula, the shapes that the trees and landscape assume, and the uncertainty of the journey all come to life within the confines of the imagination. Without the descriptive nature of lyrical content, the mind can wander and create whole new worlds that defy logic and explanation. As Shakespeare was quoted as saying in Henry V: "Upon this, your imaginary forces work."

Strange World

In many ways, "Strange World" appears to be the final piece of a trifecta of songs whose order doesn't appear to be by accident in any way. From the gothic horror that was more than present in "Phantom of the Opera," the driving force and captivating landscapes that were prevalent in "Transylvania" all come to a place of finality in "Strange World." In many ways, it returns the listener to the ethereal landscapes that were present in "Remember Tomorrow." And much like many songs of a similar nature, its interpretation is one that's completely subjective to the listener.

"The only place where you can dream. Living here is not what it seems." Immediately, this passage sets a tone of otherworldliness. In this location, reality ceases to exist, and once again, Iron Maiden allows us to embrace escapism from the harshness and monotony of the physical world. "Nobody there to reason why" alludes to a location where logic and the other deductive reasoning of our world cease to exist. "Here I am, I'm not really there" almost comes across like something from the mind of Jean-Paul Sartre, a moment of existentialism where our own role in reality is insignificant. For the lack of a better term, we finally see the "bigger picture" of things.

"I'm happy in my new strange world" displays a moment of contentment since the narrator has become completely removed from the physical reality in which he was once part. Whether this is a new spiritual existence or simply the matter of living within a dream is entirely up to personal interpretation. Going back to the Socratic method in which all things are subjective and must be questioned, the lyric "Living here, you'll never grow old" hints at living in a memory. However, some have hinted at this being an allusion to vampirism, especially with a lyrical passage that describes girls drinking plasma wine. I feel this is more of a sight that the narrator witnesses in his travels to this mysterious location. In this place, the factors that we associate with the physical world cease to exist, and we find an escape from the harsh reality that we're forced to endure.

Charlotte the Harlot

Delving into the myths and legends of Ancient Greece, one cannot help but be impressed with the detail and scope of the world in which the pantheon of gods resides. The stories and saga of Zeus and the gods of Mt. Olympus are, without question, some of the most detailed and revered legacies in the entire canon of Western literature. Mythologies have persisted ever since, whether they be the world of Middle Earth formulated by J.R.R. Tolkien, the legacy of the Dollanganger family in Flowers in the Attic by VC Andrews, and even The Hell Priest (aka Pinhead) formulated from the mind of Clive Barker.

Mythology is much more than a story. It's far more than something being created by a novelist who has an overdeveloped sense of their own creative prowess. Mythologies are vast and contain a deep world that necessitates analysis and understanding. Why do I mention this concept? Iron Maiden have formulated their own mythology that begins on the first album with the infamous "Charlotte the Harlot." It almost seems out of character for a band to formulate such an in-depth story around a sex worker, but, as had happened during the still unsolved serial murders of Jack the Ripper, sex work had been a prominent aspect in the East End of London. While some attribute the act to poverty and desperation, it's very much a reality that still exists today. The "world's oldest profession," as it's sometimes referred to, has existed in one way or another in just about every civilization.

Dave Murray might not have foreseen that his composition would become a self-contained mythology that would span over the course of four different albums. The establishment of Charlotte can not only be seen in the art that accompanies this album but also in their following release, *Killers*. A window can be seen, its red curtain the familiar tell-tale sign that the protagonist is "open for business." Remarkably, "Charlotte the Harlot" and the follow-up that would appear on *Number of the Beast* entitled "22 Acacia Avenue" take a tone that one might not expect. There's no shortage of descriptions that illustrate the actions of Charlotte being a woman of the night, especially with "Taking so many men to your room. Don't you feel no remorse? You charge them a 'fiver,' It's only for starters. And ten for the main course." The song is more akin to the pity and sadness that someone feels for any individual who tosses the value of existence away. The narrator of the song sees the self-inflicted damage of the sex trade in the East End and looks beyond the commodification of the human body to see the individual who's oppressed by the never-ending cycle of poverty.

While there's very little in the realm of philosophy that I can attribute to Murray's composition, from a purely analytical standpoint, this humanizes the sex worker and attempts to make the listener bear witness to the tragedy. We all have people in our sphere of influence who have, for lack of a better term, gone downhill. The sadness of the song is cleverly disguised in the musical composition. If there's one philosophical thought I can offer, it's that of *Justine or the Misfortunes of Virtue* by The Marquis de Sade. In de Sade's text, the titular character is humiliated again and again in a series of misadventures where she continually falls prey to those who find a way to use her naivety and strong belief in virtue against her. In some regards, Charlotte the Harlot is a tragic character as she falls victim to the circumstances of her environment. While de Sade's work has much more to do with the failings of morality taught to the masses through organized religion and the hypocrisy contained therein, Iron Maiden's song firmly establishes the desperation and despair of the East End.

Sanctuary

Now, the purpose of my discourse is to treat each album as its own separate reality and do my best to avoid events that are occurring in the modern world. That said, there have been countless artistic endeavors that serve as a direct assault on the establishment and ruling bodies of government. And it would be impossible to present any sort of discourse regarding the song "Sanctuary" and not mention the cover art that accompanied the release of the single. Once again, returning to the motif of the serial killing and preying that has occurred in the east end, as they did with "Prowler," the imagery possesses no pretense regarding its intention.

In a pose that almost seems reminiscent of Jack the Ripper's reign of terror in Whitechapel, the band's mascot,

Eddie, stands over the lifeless body of Prime Minister Margret Thatcher, a banner draped over her brandishing the now legendary Iron Maiden logo. I'll keep the explanations of the political climate in Britain as limited as possible. Still, the decade would have no shortage of artists expressing their contempt for the "Iron Lady" and her legislation through a variety of album covers that cast pretense and subversion aside in favor of unbridled hatred.

Artwork aside, "Sanctuary" doesn't contain any hints at the political climate aside from its confrontational artwork. That said, it reflects the violent crime of the East End, this time from the narrative point of view of a fugitive. "I've never killed a woman before, but I know how it feels.

I know you'd have gone insane. If you saw what I saw, now I have to look for sanctuary from the law." Reveals the shift in psychology that comes with criminal sociopathy. It's a telling song that coincides with "Running Free" and the self-titled song that immediately follows it. Crime thrives in poverty and locations that are worn down due to economic hardships. Repurposing the fugitive in the run and the prowler stalking the night to represent a band going against the tide of societal expectations is something that we'll see throughout the decade. For anyone populating the working-class areas of London, it's certainly identifiable.

The criminal mind has long been a source of fascination for many. In fact, one could even draw a parallel between this mindset and the ambition that comes with the unrelenting desire to succeed. While both have very different ambitions and goals, both of them have the mindset of operating outside the confines of society and what's deemed permissible and socially acceptable.

Iron Maiden

There's something to be said about the willingness to create any form of art and display it to the world. While artists will insist that they don't pay attention to what the masses think about them, there is a feeling of wanting to be observed as adept at your particular craft and have others take it as seriously as you do. This brings me to one of the few instances in which a self-titled song appears on a self-titled album that's named after the band who composed and played it. As a song, "Iron Maiden" is a fierce declaration of intent from a band who might have been a genuine and definitive product of the East End but had their sights set on things that would eventually take them far beyond it.

When we break down the meaning of what an Iron Maiden is, a coffin filled with spikes meant to encapsulate a victim and impale them, there's no better name for a group who were taking their first steps toward domination. While one might assume that a self-titled song of this nature might be a simple expose of violence that tended to be associated with the device in question, the song takes a different approach. It serves as a declarative statement by the band.

While there's no denying that there's a predatory element in the lyrical approach, in particular with the passage

"I just want to see your blood, I just want to stand and stare," this could easily be deduced as an allusion to being held in awe by the spectacle that stands before them. "Iron Maiden can't be fought; Iron Maiden can't be sought" is straight and to the point. There's very little in the way of a philosophical discourse to be had. There is no pretense, just the unrelenting determination of a band who has their sights set on conquering the world before them. "Iron Maiden wants you for dead." The battle cry that, in just a few short years, would take the world by storm and become a self-fulfilling prophecy.

The Stage is Set, and The Magician is Ready…

When the magician approaches the altar to change the course of events beyond the scope of reality, they know that there is always a necessity for the right implements, tools, and a balance between the elements that make up the world. To say that all of these elements were certainly present on the debut Iron Maiden album would certainly be an understatement. The poise and purpose that was certainly present were only going to become more refined as the group honed and sharpened their craft. It's only fitting that we end this first part of this discourse from the band themselves, all of whom are certainly adepts in their own right: "Iron Maiden's going to get you!"

Killers (1981): The Underbelly of the East End & Ascension

Engaging in any discourse regarding art presents a difficulty. This is especially true when the discussion relates to the collective efforts of a group whose work spans multiple years. Pinpointing just one album as their most remarkable is an even greater challenge. How do you make a selection that stands above everything else? All art is subjective, and perspective exists on a broad spectrum based entirely on individual analysis. Regarding the albums of Iron Maiden, I have to separate personal preference from overriding quality. And yet, it's somewhat of an easy choice for me to make. That album is *Killers*.

It's impossible to go any further regarding this particular era of the band without mentioning the contributions of two individuals who would both play pivotal roles in shaping Iron Maiden's upward trajectory for the rest of the decade. The first was Adrian Smith, who replaced Dennis Stratton on guitar. Smith would remain with the band for the rest of the decade and return in the early 2000s on one of the band's most significant releases, *Brave New World*.

Some of Smith's most notable contributions would occur outside of Iron Maiden during the 1990s, on two of Bruce Dickinson's solo albums, *Accident of Birth* and *The Chemical Wedding*. Dickinson's solo material has always had peaks and valleys regarding quality. For instance, *Tattooed Millionaire,* which would also feature future Maiden guitarist Janick Gers, was heavily laden with catchy hooks and a bit of snarky English wit in the case of the album's title track. Other releases like *Skunkworks* attempted to adapt to changing commercial trends.

Perhaps the most notable change during this time period relates to who was working behind the scenes: producer Martin Birch. This partnership would be influential in taking the band to the next level and delving deep into realms that might have been impossible up to this point.

Much of the subject matter depicted in *Killers* is still very much inspired by the environment of London's East End. That said, it also indicates a band progressing in their composition and having the ability to project new ideas and explore new frontiers. The material grew in prowess and presentation, and the lyrical content showed a growth and maturity far ahead of where the group had been just one year before.

While this would be the beginning of a lengthy partnership with Adran Smith and Martin Birch, it was the beginning of the end of another era, as it would be the final album with frontman Paul Di'Anno. The seismic shift that would occur because of this is unquestionable. Much like the magician at his altar, the new reality that would manifest would be both extraordinary and otherworldly.

The cover art that had adorned the band's previous release contained subtle hints regarding the degeneration and darkness associated with London's East End. The artwork for *Killers* contains nothing in the way of pretense in illustrating the history of violent crime that has accompanied poverty and desperation. The image of Eddie holding a blood-soaked hatchet with a sadistic grin on his face as the hands of his recently dispatched victim cling to his shirt captures this bleak reality. While the transgression and brutality of album covers have continued to evolve, the artwork adorning *Killers* remains a masterclass in allowing the imagination to wonder what might have occurred just moments before. As I've remarked several times throughout my career as a film critic, real horror is what one doesn't see.

If the albums of Iron Maiden each possess their own reality, then *Killers* is an unflinching look into the darker side of the human experience. Embodying the mythology that the band had begun with their previous release, a silhouette of "Charlotte the Harlot" can be seen in the foreground, her red curtains signaling another night when she's open for business.

The blackened sky on the cover is a brooding sight, and the fact that a streetlamp is the only source of illumination implies that the only rays of hope for the residents of the East End are artificial. In the background is the Ruskin Arms, a tavern where Iron Maiden spent their formative years. Everything that finds its way onto the cover of *Killers* represents a contrast between the journey the band had embarked upon and the fabricated reality they had begun to formulate. This is a metaphysical example where both worlds become intertwined in a single plane of existence.

The Ides of March

"Cowards die many times before their deaths;
The valiant never taste of death but once."
-William Shakespeare, Julius Caesar, Act Two, Scene 2

Julius Caesar, the general who had subdued Gaul and waged civil war on Rome to achieve his ambitions. From his exploits on the battlefield and consolidation of control within the corridors of power, Caesar's life is one of ambition and methodical calculation. Even his writings paint the picture of a ruthless tactician who understood the power of propaganda through the written word.

There's an excellent chance that Caesar's military career and his control over Rome would still be well known in academic circles; they also might have been relegated to textbooks had it not been for the play written by Shakespeare. The words composed by the bard have now entered the lexicon of popular culture, such as "friends, Romans, countrymen, lend me your ears," "Et Tu Brute?" and "Cry havoc and let slip the dogs of war" have all found their way into several films and stories throughout the years.

The 'Ides of March,' or March 15th, refers to a warning issued to Caesar in the play by a soothsayer, telling him to beware of this date. As it turns out, this marked the day of his assassination. There are reports that Caesar knew of his impending fate, even declining a personal bodyguard and remarking that "it is better to die once than live forever in fear of death."

Naming the opening instrumental track after this famous harbinger of destruction that's embedded deep within the public consciousness, Iron Maiden establishes what is about to follow. This will be a grandiose experience about to be told that will weave the listener into a complex tapestry.

"The Ides of March" catapults the listener into the fray. Similar to the introduction that the Marquis de Sade issues the reader in *The 120 Days of Sodom* or the witch utters in *At Midnight I'll Take Your Soul,* we're assured that there's no turning back from this point forward. As Dante Alighieri wrote in the Divine Comedy hundreds of years ago, "Abandon all hope, ye who enter here."

Wrathchild

The dust barely settles from the pummeling instrumental, and then "Wrathchild" thrusts us into personal turmoil. In "Wrathchild," we're once again relegated to the realm of the perpetual inner struggle of the outsider. There are two ways one could look at "Wrathchild." If we take a straightforward approach and critique it simply based on the narrator's perspective, we see an inner struggle based on previous trauma.

The narrator, who describes himself as "never meant to be" and never knowing his father, lacks any sense of self or identity, that is, literally being a "Wrathchild," born into a "scene of angriness and greed…dominance and persecution." The title alone can refer to being born out of a violent scenario, such as a sexual assault, that is, being bred out of a tumultuous situation and not consensual reproduction. The search is all-consuming, with the narrator remarking that if he's unsuccessful, the search will lead to him "going crazy."

> "And now I spend my time looking all around
> For a man that's nowhere to be found
> Until I find him, I'm never gonna stop searching
> I'm gonna find my man, gonna travel around."

That's one way of interpreting the material that we're presented with. We can see this as examining the physical reality of the song's narrator. But let's take a further look into the plight of what the narrator is experiencing. We see something that might not have been an intention when Steve Harris penned the lyrics but indeed shed light on something psychologists have discussed throughout the years: human beings being products of their environment.

The psychologist who determines that a person's environment has led to their behaviors and the magician whose intuition deduces the spiritual degeneration of an individual are merely two perspectives that exist to provide an explanation. Those adept in psychology and students of the esoteric are simply agreeing on identical concepts, albeit worded slightly differently.

"Ain't nothin' gonna alter the course of my destination. I know I've got to find some serious piece of mind, or I know I'll just go crazy" certainly implies the basic obsession that's a part of human nature and the self-awareness that describes the necessity of closure with trauma. Perhaps our narrator knows that his situation is a cause for his behavior and is knowledgeable about his fixation on accomplishing the task at hand. Perhaps this represents a deeper aspect of something being a lost cause, yet the obsession to "keep on searching" is addictive.

Murders in the Rue Morgue

Few writers have captivated the imagination and the darker aspects of human nature more than Edgar Allan Poe. His tales of the macabre have made a remarkable impact on multiple generations, and their influence can be seen in a wide range of artistic mediums. There are many different adaptations to stage and screen by those mesmerized by tales that journey to the far reaches of the imagination and embrace the morbid atmosphere that accompanies death.

"Murders in the Rue Morgue" is one of the many tales in which a complex mystery is woven around a murder, with deduction and reasoning utilized to solve the case. Since the publication of Poe's titular work, the fascination with such stories has persisted to the present day. The public has found a way to lose themselves in the master skills of fictional detectives such as Sherlock Holmes and Hercule Poirot. They provide an escape from the mundane and allow readers to immerse themselves in intrigue and mystery.

While not a direct adaptation of Poe's literary work, Iron Maiden's composition is a defining example of the group developing their skills in world-building. The listener is taken away to a place separate from our basic conception of reality. Much like the magician at the altar, this is created through ritual and ceremony, albeit with instrumentation and captivating lyrics.

> "I remember it as plain as day
> Although it happened in the dark of the night
> I was strolling' through the streets of Paris
> And it was cold it was starting to rain
> And then I heard a piercing scream
> And I rushed to the scene of the crime
> But all I found was the butchered remains
> Of two girls lay side by side."

From the opening verse, the narrator takes us to the rain-soaked streets of Paris. The night obscures the sights on the street but not the memory of the experience. The lyrical content and musical arrangement paint a unique landscape; the rain and scream piercing the night all seem reminiscent of Jack the Ripper's crimes in Whitechapel. This scenario could have easily occurred and illustrates that reality and fiction aren't as far apart as we might think.

The events of the song unfold like a Giallo film or thriller. The delivery is what elevates their realism to the point of being identifiable. After all, these tales are full of ordinary individuals who wind up in extraordinary situations. The truth is obscured to the audience, so much the better.

The extraordinary situation in the song involves a case of mistaken identity, with the narrator being forced to go on the run due to his lack of ability to speak French and the Gendarmes believing he's the culprit. Carrying on the theme of the nomad on the run from forces that represent the establishment, Murders in the Rue Morgue takes this theme in a new direction that allows the group to simultaneously embrace the classics of literature and how they can relate to modern sensibilities. This trend will be carried on in subsequent releases.

Now, I could dive deeper and compare Poe's original story to the song, but I firmly believe you should seek out the source material.

Another Life

At this point in their ever-developing career, Iron Maiden had written about criminals and the outer fringe in terms of representing their ambition to escape a cycle of poverty and violence that have been associated with the East End of London. Iron Maiden were undoubtedly not the first group to romanticize these struggles, and "Another Life" represents a different aspect altogether.

Living outside the rigid confines that mainstream society places upon the masses has always been alluring for many. The willingness to defy societal expectations and possess personal autonomy over ourselves is one of the driving aspects that first piqued my interest in philosophy.

"Another Life" explores this mindset, and the structure of the song represents the repetitive nature in which mental illness sometimes occurs within the mind of the individual. From Nietzsche to Van Gogh, insanity has plagued some of the most talented minds. "Another Life" represents this inner turmoil and the struggle of whether or not to continue existing.

> "As I lay here, lying on my bed
> Sweet voices come into my head
> Oh, what is it? I wanna know
> Please, won't you tell me, it's got to go
> There's a feeling that's inside me
> Telling me to get away
> But I'm so tired of living
> I might as well end today."

The narrator of the song lives in a comatose state in which psychosis plays a dominant role. The previously mentioned verse are the only lyrics to be found within the entire song. The fact that this verse is repeated three times shows the monotony of the narrator's plight. There's more to the outer fringe than romanticizing life on the edge. From a philosophical standpoint, it's the concept of duality. The complex struggles between logic and emotion make the will to continue difficult.

Logic can be seen in the narrator recognizing his dementia and the presence of voices in his head. At the opposite end of the spectrum, the intense emotions of wanting to give up and the frustrations that occur through melancholy clash with the knowledge of his manias.

An aspect we take away from this is that those who choose "another life" that's different from our own still suffer through the monotony of existence. They don't always find personal satisfaction and contentment. While the stigma of mental health is still prominent even today, this gives us a glimpse into the mindset that so many people have struggled with for centuries.

Genghis Khan

"The greatest happiness is to vanquish your enemies, to chase them before you, to rob them of their wealth, to see those dear to them bathed in tears, to clasp to your bosom their wives and daughters."

-Genghis Khan

One of the most challenging tasks I have in front of me is providing any sort of in-depth analysis when it comes to instrumental tracks. An album cover usually sets the tone for what the listener can expect, and lyrical content is part and parcel of telling a story and conveying a deeper meaning to the audience.

"Genghis Khan" and "The Ides of March" are examples of detailed visual storytelling, albeit with instrumentation that captivates the listener's imagination. Closing your eyes allows you to visualize the Mongol hordes galloping across the countryside, subduing enemies, and disappearing as quickly as they attack.

If "Transylvania" captures the brooding atmosphere of gothic horror, and "The Ides of March" sets the tone for what's to follow, then "Genghis Khan" resting between "Another Life" and "Innocent Exile" is a reprieve from the songs on the album that deals with the inner turmoil of existence.

By capturing the imagination, our perception sharpens, and we're prepared to continue a journey without a specific destination. Yet, simultaneously, we travel to many different worlds that we've never experienced before, except in the manufactured reality of art.

Innocent Exile

One of the dominant themes throughout *Killers* is the study of individuals who reside in the underbelly of society and their struggles. Be it the environment that creates them or, in the case of "Innocent Exile," a false accusation. From the most basic of critiques, it might be assumed that this could be a continuation of "Murders in the Rue Morgue." After all, both songs deal with the aspect of accusations of an innocent party being presumed guilty of a violent crime. However, the two have a gulf of differences, which I shall attempt to make more noticeable.

"Murders in the Rue Morgue" contains a considerable emphasis on storytelling that focuses on placing the viewer into the streets of Paris, down to the narrator recounting how vivid his memories are, describing the streets being soaked with rain and the piercing cry that breaks the stillness of the calm night. "Innocent Exile" is more ambiguous with its narrative approach. That is to say; the details make the listener aware that the narrator has been accused of a violent crime and is on the run from the law.

"My life is so empty, nothing to live for
My mind is all confusion, 'cause I defied the law
When you weren't there to help me, I lost my mind and ran
I never had no trouble before this all began, yeah."

The lyrical phrasing of the song in question has more in common with that of "Another Life," as the first two verses repeat themselves. The lyrical passage "My life is so empty, nothing to live for. My mind is all confused, 'cause I defied the law," establishes the hopelessness of the narrator's situation, and the repetitive nature hints at the monotony that comes with being "on the lamb."

Once again, this storytelling allows the listener to use their imagination and determine what sequence of events led up to the situation being described and what the future might be for the fugitive on the run. A significant aspect of ritual and ceremony is to form a reality in the mind's eye. This is the nature of metaphysics in art; we're forced to take a deeper look at what we're presented with and formulate introspection through imagination.

Killers

The criminal behavior that has sometimes become synonymous with the East End is vividly displayed on the album's title track. The material presented so far has touched upon the mental illness that might inflict the outer fringe as well as the plight of false accusations. "Killers" takes things in another direction that not only examines the predatory nature of evil but also the compulsion that accompanies the sociopathy of serial murder, so much so that the lyrical delivery of the song splits its narrative between two perspectives, albeit from the same individual.

Earlier on, we established the aspect of Iron Maiden developing their craft further in building new worlds with their musical arrangements and lyrical content. On the title track, both of these aspects are on full display. Much like the tension that builds up from a killer stalking their prey, the brooding pacing of the song gradually builds up during the introduction. The bass line from Steve Harris, in particular, almost mimics the footsteps of someone slowly approaching from behind. Then, as if the calm before the storm has ended and the gates of hell have opened wide, a barrage of drums and guitar break the monotony as victim and assailant begin their dance of death. The opening verse has a third-person perspective that sets the tone immediately. This presentation almost seems like the duality of a mindset that's associated with psychopathy.

"You walk through the subway
His eyes burn a hole in your back
A footstep behind you
He lunges prepared for attack."

The narrator talks about the cold-blooded murderer who awaits in the shadows, looking for the perfect opportunity to strike his quarry. Then, the narrator discusses his intention from a first-person perspective. This illustrates the duality within those who creep silently in the darkness and the shadows, the individual who obscures himself from sight, and the person gripped by the compulsion of sociopathy to strike out against their victims.

"My innocent victims
Are slaughtered with wrath and despise
The mocking religion
Of hatred that burns in the night."

This depiction of opposites exists more clearly in the lyrical phrasing of the opening verse. "You walk through the subway. My eyes burn a hole in your back" recounts the same situation, but the narrator sees himself in the scenario. No longer observing the situation, the narrator loses control and surrenders to compulsion.

"My faith in believing
Is stronger than lifelines and ties
The glimmer of metal
My moment is ready to strike
The death call arises
A scream breaks the still of the night
Another tomorrow
Remember to walk in the light
I have found you
And now there is no place to run
Excitement shakes me
Oh God help me, what have I done?
I've done it again."

With the narrator having a moment where he realizes the fact that he's committed murder, one can't help but think of Joe Spinell's iconic performance from *Maniac* a year earlier. Bill Lustig's film balances the psychosis of a sociopath and the blight of life in an urban area. At the same time, there's an attempt to live in the world while projecting a relative state of normalcy. As we've seen in the cases of serial killers such as John Wayne Gacy, Ted Bundy, and even BTK, these monsters among us are adept at being the ultimate wolf in sheep's clothing, blending into societal norms but having a completely different persona as it relates to others compulsion to commit murder.

"Killers" represent the duality of human nature. The thin line that exists between the compulsion of addiction and sociopathy and the knowledge that an act is wrong and carnal. And while I've mentioned Jack the Ripper multiple times throughout the discourse of these first two releases, the "glimmer of metal" is eerily similar to an anonymous letter sent in during the killing spree in Whitechapel in which someone claiming to be the ripper stated that his "knife was nice and sharp." Killers details the intricacies of a criminal mind and focus inward to grant us a perspective of those who walk among us and are driven by impulses that repulse us to our very core.

Prodigal Son

If something can be remarked about "Prodigal Son" as a song, it's somewhat prophetic as to the new frontiers and worlds that Iron Maiden would explore on subsequent releases. That is to say, Steve Harris' expansive knowledge of literature, history, folklore, and mythology would allow the songwriter to weave complex narratives that would introduce listeners to a brave new world that exists beyond the confines of an album.

I intend to confine this discourse to each album and treat them like their own reality, separate from the physical one we exist within. I mention this to explore the song "Prodigal Son" so that mythology becomes inexplicably linked to the nature of evil within the album itself.

What strikes me as most fascinating is that the title, one of the main characters that the narrator of the song addresses, and the content are a trifecta of varying opposites. The term 'Prodigal Son' refers to a part of the Gospel According to St. Luke. The story speaks of a young man who asks for his inheritance and, after squandering it upon a life of embellishments and indulgence, is reduced to a life of poverty.

The aspect of the prodigal son returning is an expression that's found its way into our modern dialogue. This terminology usually refers to a black sheep departing to participate in activities and events that are met with disapproval or condemnation and then a reunion where forgiveness is asked for.

Despite the Prodigal Son being an aspect emanating from the New Testament of the Holy Bible, the song makes no mention of the scriptures, nor does it allude to Christianity in any way, except for the song's narrator mentioning that the "Devil's got a hold of my soul, and he won't just let it be."

While the song's narrator pleads to Lamia, a figure of Greek mythology and not one associated with the New Testament, the aspect of understanding the error of one's ways and the repercussions that follow are more than noticeable throughout the song.

According to legend, Lamia was a queen once beloved by Zeus. When Hera took the children the two had together from her, she degenerated into a demoness who spent her days devouring children, seducing men, and murdering them. Much like the legend that many would use regarding the gypsies as thieves of children, Lamia became known as a folk legend to instill fear into young children in Ancient Greece to behave. The mellow atmosphere of the song and its placement right after the album's title track is a unique choice, as it provides the bearing of a guilty conscience and recognition of personal failure.

"Listen to me Lamia, listen to what I've got to say
I've got these feelings and they won't go away
I've got these fears inside that bring me to my knees
Oh, help me Lamia or I'm sure I'll die, oh please
I feel unsettled now, I know that I've done wrong
Messed around with mystic things and magic for far too long
I feel I'm being paid with this nightmare inside me
The devil's got a hold on my soul and he just won't let me be."

The amalgamation of these different variables makes for an intriguing song and, in its own way, illustrates the similarities between psychology, religion, and esoteric thinking. The narrator, "possessed" by thoughts that he attributes to the devil after experimentation with "mystic things and magic," could refer to sorcery or substance abuse, as these have similar outcomes that end in self-destruction.

Many of the terms used in spiritual circles have their direct equivalent in modern psychology. Linking them together in the context of the song forces us to look a little deeper at the world of metaphysics.

One aspect of demonology is that demons can be interpreted as different vices that are practiced by human beings. Perhaps the narrator recognizes his errors in exploring the nether regions of the abyss, a moment where the realization of his error arrives too late to correct.

Purgatory

A common theme that you'll see repeated several times throughout this discourse is the concept of duality. Whether it's darkness or light, the microcosm and macrocosm, or the comparison of the reality we experience physically or spiritually. This concept is a cornerstone of philosophical thought and exists within the confines of the song Purgatory.

Before I continue my discourse on this song in particular, some context needs to be explained regarding the concept of Purgatory itself. While the concepts of heaven and hell have always existed in one form or another as ways to give some sort of depiction of the afterlife, certain religions depict a purification place before the soul continues its journey onward, moving in the form of Purgatory.

Described in vivid detail in Dante Aligieri's The Divine Comedy, Dante promoted the idea of not being a place where individuals atone for their sins but take time to reflect on their behaviors and correct them. This aspect of self-realization and enlightenment can be attributed to both dogmatic principles and the modern field of psychology.

Both practices have common ground in Dante's description of purgatory, that self-realization and modification of destructive behaviors are universal processes. This is practiced by both neophytes of any esoteric philosophy or an individual who's seeking psychological or psychiatric help. As for the song that made its way onto the Iron Maiden album we're currently discussing, duality is at the forefront of the lyrical content.

While I intend to keep many of the themes of this discourse confined to a single reality that the album presents, "Purgatory" itself is very reminiscent of "Electric Caravan" by Black Sabbath, where the narrator recounts his experiences in entering a reality that is wholly divorced from the physical one that we all exist in.

> "Thinking of an age, old dream
> Places I have never seen
> Fantasies lived times before
> I split my brain, melt through the floor
> Over clouds, my mind will fly
> Forever now, I can't think why
> My body tries to leave my soul
> Is it me? I just don't know."

The concept of the narrator "splitting his brain," which some have alluded to as the usage of hallucinogenic drugs, has a much deeper meaning when we take the words at a literal value. The human brain has been well documented as having two opposing sides, one that thrives on logic and the other emotion. Let's take the lyrical passage literally. We're led to assume that both sides of the brain work in unison to take the narrator on a journey into the mind where the future, past, and present coexist perfectly.

Drifter

Many have remarked over the years that *Killers* is a perfect album from start to finish. I'm quite inclined to agree with this sentiment. The ebb and flow of the songs, the lyrical themes that probe a multitude of subject material, and the compositions that show impeccable attention to detail make *Killers* an iconic album that would pave the way for several others to follow in its footsteps.

Just as important as an album's opening track, grasps the listener's attention and establishes the material that's bound to follow, is the final track on the album that, in many ways, can either be a coup de gras or a harbinger of future events to come. The ideal conclusion manifests itself in *Killers* in "Drifter," a perfect closer if there ever was one. "Drifter" once again sees Iron Maiden going to the well and displaying the actions of the individual who operates on their terms.

"What do you feel when you hold me tight?
I'm gonna cuddle up to you tonight
Gonna get you feeling so secure
Listen, child, don't you see there's a cure?

ooh, yeah
Anyway, got to get you away
Feels so good, think it's gonna be a new day."

A mundane analysis might interpret the lyrics as nothing more than the hedonistic actions of someone who, for lack of a better term, loves them and leaves them. This is an easy assumption to make, as it's been a topic repeated many times. I'm never one to take any artistic endeavor at face value. I see something else within the lyrical content in "Drifter" that's more representative of the band as a whole and not someone looking to get their rocks off and move on to a new conquest.

"Drifter" has much more in common with the collective goal of a band looking to always take that next step in their career and not be complacent with their current status. "I've gotta keep on roaming gotta sing my song" can easily be interpreted as going from town to town and touring. It would be easy to assume that the song is simply about partaking in the local female residents, but being a drifter is all part and parcel to being on the road as a band.

Drifter almost comes across as a prophetic statement regarding where Iron Maiden would go next. They would indeed keep roaming on and singing their song, several of them. Based on what we know through the power of hindsight, we can now look at "Drifter" as a self-fulfilling prophecy as to what the rest of the decade would bring.

The End of the Beginning

There are many reasons why so many individuals, me included, would regard *Killers* as the definitive Iron Maiden album. I hope that what I've brought forth in terms of discourse has allowed this theory to be reinforced. While this would be the end of one particular era in the ever-growing legacy of Iron Maiden, in many ways, it was the beginning of another era that would surpass the expectations of many and quite possibly the band themselves.

In an alternate form of history, one more album with Paul Di'Anno up front would have seen the band go in a direction that further enveloped their roots in the East End and explored darker subject matter. Of course, as we'll soon find out, this was not meant to be. Di'Anno's departure would see Iron Maiden travel in new directions with a new voice, a new album, and the beginnings of a new legacy that would see them be catapulted into the highest echelons of the genre. Still, few moments in their career have been more flawless and poised than *Killers*. But the band would soon outgrow their humble beginnings and environment, and the world was ripe for the taking.

The Number of the Beast (1982): A New Voice

A common factor unites artists, students of the esoteric, and anyone else with a vision or goal for themselves: the necessity for progression and development. The writer who strives to sharpen his skills, the magician who strives to understand the secrets obscured by the high priestess, and any musician changing their direction and evolving their craft into a force of nature to be reckoned with.

It was inevitable that Iron Maiden would outgrow London's East End. In every concept of the phrase, *The Number of the Beast* shows Iron Maiden developing a new voice, and not just because of the introduction of new vocalist Bruce Dickinson. While the sound of the band was growing exponentially, this would be a remarkable turning point in terms of the subject matter that they would start exploring. The first two albums were authentic depictions of the poverty-stricken existence of life in the East End. Now, much like the person who comes of age and leaves their place of birth, there are new places to journey to, new areas to explore, and a world to win. Iron Maiden were poised for this journey.

Let us take nothing away from the accomplishments of Paul Di'Anno. His cockney swagger and vocal delivery were major factors in allowing Iron Maiden to establish a foothold responsible for their upward trajectory for the rest of the decade. When it came to aggression and angst and emerging from such a poverty-stricken area, Di'Anno was the ideal voice to encapsulate such an environment. As Iron Maiden began to build more complex worlds and apply their trade to in-depth storytelling, a voice such as Bruce Dickinson's was essential for facilitating these journeys into new frontiers.

The material on *Number of the Beast* embraced various new topics, from facets of British pop culture ("Children of the Damned," "The Prisoner"), history ("Invaders," "Run to the Hills"), and alternate realities that were closely intertwined with the one that we exist in ("22 Acacia Avenue," "Hallowed Be Thy Name," "Gangland.") And, of course, the album's title track would emerge from a dreamscape and later be subject to misinterpretation from the uninitiated.

From a philosophical standpoint, *Number of the Beast* is the equivalent of the neophyte obtaining a form of enlightenment. It's the moment when awareness of a broader spectrum of reality is achieved. The world is seen as much more than just what is presented before our eyes, and we can, for the lack of a better term, see the bigger picture of the matter. This broader horizon of this new perspective is certainly present within the album's cover art, which is more fantastic and grandiose than the first two previous albums had been.

As further proof that the group had outgrown the dark streets of the East End that had once been home to Jack the Ripper, the city's aesthetic was abandoned. The band's mascot, Eddie, stands over a barren landscape, holding an almost comical representation of the devil in the strings of a marionette. The devil holds his own marionette of Eddie above a fiery landscape with human bodies carefully woven into the firestorm, courtesy of artist Derek Riggs' skilled hand.

The artwork poses the question of who's really in control of destiny. Do we possess personal autonomy, with deities merely being man-made fabrications to exert control, or is there a higher intelligence that guides our fate that we don't have the capability to comprehend? Analysis of the artwork itself is a two-fold endeavor that comes in the form of whether someone sees the glass as half-empty or half-full. For the pessimist they might see the artwork depicting the control that one has over one's own fate as being delusional, as the devil wields control over our destiny. For the optimist and the interpretation, I take from Riggs' artwork, something else is suggested that speaks to the band's ambition.

The image of Eddie wielding the strings shows the band firmly in control of their own destiny, even outmaneuvering any outside forces that were there to hinder their rise to prominence. All art is subjective, and because the best creations come from a place of selfishness or self-interest on behalf of the individual, we can look at the artwork as a statement of intent.

Invaders

If you turn back the pages of history, you'll see evidence supporting the theory that truth is more incredible than fiction. In the rich history connected with the British Isles, there's an almost never-ending lineage of material from which to draw inspiration. Be it the centuries-old monarchy, the Victorian age, the days of heroes such as Horatio Nelson and the Duke of Wellington, or the rich literary canon that extends from Shakespeare to Matthew Lewis, Charles Dickens, and Sir Walter Scott.

And it's the age before monarchy or the glory days of Britannia that "Invaders" takes place in. The clash between the Saxons and Nordic tribesmen is the area that Harris chooses to explore. While the history of the British military is full of victories against insurmountable odds, many of which have been immortalized in films such as *Zulu*, "Invaders" is rather honest about how the Saxon tribes fall in the face of the Norsemen.

The Vikings first attacked England in 793, sacking a church and being described as "bringing ruin and slaughter." The Viking attacks continued over the next few centuries, establishing multiple strongholds in Northern England. There would even be four Viking kings who ruled England from 1013 to 1042. 1066, the same year as the Norman Conquest, would be the final Viking invasion. Although it had been thwarted, the exhausted English army would fall at the battle of Hastings, with William of Normandy becoming the new king of England.

"Invaders" can be seen as repurposing a historical topic to represent a band's ambition for greatness. "We cannot fight this battle alone" can even be interpreted as the band and their fan base being one and success requiring their assistance.

"The smell of death and burning flesh, the battle-weary fight to the end. The Saxons have been overpowered victims of the mighty Norsemen" are lyrics that speak to one of the song's biggest attributes, the descriptive nature. Rather than just recounting facts, the song places the listener in the forefront of the battle as the Saxons fight a losing effort. While many different artists have followed this example, Iron Maiden's opening salvo decimates the senses with its vivid descriptions and frenetic pacing and is completely unrelenting in its delivery. Both the composition and lyrical content attest to the raw power that heavy metal and armed conflict share with one another.

Like "The Ides of March" on *Killers,* "Invaders" establishes a template for the rest of the album. We will be taken on a journey that ebbs and flows and takes all sorts of new directions, all formulated by the band.

Children of the Damned

Aside from the rich historical lineage closely associated with England, a rich palate of film and popular culture exists. Both aspects are explored in *The Number of the Beast*. In the years following the Second World War, the efforts of many filmmakers took on a subversive art form. Horror and Science Fiction mirrored the looming threat of the Cold War, with aliens taking the place of the perceived communist threat of invasion. The red scare and the "red planet" of Mars were almost too perfect for filmmakers to take advantage of.

The most popular offerings from England during this time were from Hammer Studios, which breathed new life and rich color into gothic monsters such as Frankenstein, Dracula, and the Mummy. Aside from these gothic tales, other offerings, such as *City of the Dead,* transformed the quiet countryside into breeding grounds for a new host of nightmares. While horror has always provided a form of escapism, the subversive tone of horror coming to the sleeping hamlets and English countryside implies that nowhere was truly safe in a world that was teetering further towards self-destruction.

And this is where "Children of the Damned" takes us to.

Named for the film of the same name and its predecessor, "Village of the Damned," both films take the concept of an invading menace set against the backdrop of cold-war paranoia. Children with telekinetic abilities penetrate deep into the inner fears of the characters in the film and the audience. It's the phobia of an unseen force from those who walk among us that both films capture almost too perfectly and certainly play upon the fears of spies and those who aren't what they might seem to be.

While the Cold War was certainly still ongoing at the time of *The Number of the Beast,* the paranoia of a communist takeover of the Western world had long since subsided; the themes of destruction and dread are interwoven into the song, and the arrangements complement the lyrical content that's apocalyptic in nature.

"He's walking like a small child
But watch his eyes burn you away
Black holes in his golden stare
God knows he wants to go home."

While it would be quite simple to critique "Children of the Damned" as nothing more than something based on an aspect of popular culture, there is more to the song than what's on the surface. In continuing one of the major topics that were present on *Killers,* "Children of the Damned" taps into the predatory nature of evil. With the song being about children, who are usually thought of as innocent and non-threatening, the aspect of a predator operating in plain sight and having an unassuming form is established.

Smiles as the flame sears his flesh
Melting his face, screaming' in pain
Peeling the skin from his eyes
Watch him die according to plan
He's dust on the ground; what did we learn?

While the descriptions of death certainly exist within the realms of horror and science fiction, the aspect of those who walk among us posing a significant threat exists at the very core of the material. The nature of evil is deeply embedded in philosophy, most notably from Immanuel Kant.

Kant formulated the theory that humans have a natural propensity for evil when we "subordinate the law for our own self-interest." This argument can certainly be seen as a supportive theory regarding narcissism and sociopathy, which exist at the very core of self-interest and lack of empathy for those who are victimized.

While the concepts of good and evil are sometimes thought of as well-defined by our moral compass, "Children of the Damned" displays the cold and calculating action of those who possess a predatory nature. "Smiles as the flame sears his flesh" implies sadism and knowledge of the vindictive actions that one is performing. Autonomy and free will used for one's own purposes is something vividly depicted in Kant's writings, and it certainly finds its way into "Children of the Damned."

The Prisoner

We go from one staple of British popular culture to another, although this time, we travel from the big screen to the smaller one, with "The Prisoner." While the scope and presentation of television programs have changed significantly over the years, some programs still incite thought and conversation from viewers who wish to escape the confines of reality. *The Prisoner* is one of these. The driving force behind the series was its star, Patrick McGoohan.

It would be a daunting challenge to dissect and analyze the entire series. Like *Eraserhead* and *El Topo, The Prisoner* is subject to many different interpretations. So much so that, like *Eraserhead,* if six different people were asked their thoughts on the subject, you might have six different answers.

The saga of a resigned agent living in a community where people are assigned numbers and tracked down by floating objects certainly provides some insight into contemporary society's views of the populace. "I am not a number. I am a free man!" speaks to our desire to embrace our identity and exist as a wolf among the endless throngs of sheep.

For this reason, *The Prisoner* is the perfect subject material for the band to focus on. From an artistic standpoint, the band, which was still developing and finding its own unique voice, championed a series that told the story of someone who strived to be free and not categorized by convenient definitions, striking a chord with human nature.

From a philosophical point of view, the ascension of consciousness elevates an individual above the complacency of the herd. For example, The Book of the Law states that "every man and woman is a star." Despite Crowley alluding to us as beacons of light shining bright as a collective body, we're still a collective body where "every number is infinite; there is no difference." To shine brighter than those around us and to gain something that makes us unique is at the core of many esoteric and philosophical teachings.

The song's lyrical content echoes both perspectives almost too perfectly. "Break down the walls, I'm coming out" and "Do what I want and do what I please" are instantly identifiable to anyone lusting for freedom. One doesn't have to be familiar with the television series to feel empowered.

"If you kill me, it's self-defense

if I kill you, then I call it vengeance
Spit in your eye; I will defy
You'll be afraid when I call out your name
Echoing strength, passion, and the quest to be free, The Prisoner speaks to the individual and outsider in us all."

22 Acacia Avenue

While Iron Maiden had outgrown the East End at this juncture in their career, the desire to escape from poverty and violence is still expressed thoroughly in "22 Acacia Avenue." The second installment in the self-contained mythology of "Charlotte the Harlot" is an impressive development in lyrical content and composition from the previous outing on their self-titled debut. And while the lyrics recount the similar story of a sex worker in the East End and the desperate pleas to her to escape the life she's created for herself, a slight subtext certainly calls back to the band's formative years. Within the pleas exists a desire to escape poverty and the never-ending cycle of degeneration in the area. It's fitting for the song's narrator to describe her hardship and an argument to leave her lifestyle behind.

"Beat her, mistreat her, do anything that you please
Bite her, excite her, make her get down on her knees
Abuse her, misuse her; she can take all that you've got
Caress her, molest her. She always does what you want."

The aforementioned lyrical passages depict the commodification of the human body and the lengths Charlotte goes to in order to sustain her self-destructive lifestyle. The pleas for her to reform come from desperation and despair over her situation.

"You're running away, don't you know what you're doing?
Can't you see it'll lead you to ruin?
Charlotte, you've taken your life, and you've thrown it away
You believe that because what you're earning?
Your life's good, don't you know that it's hurting?
All the people that love you, don't cast them aside
All the men that are constantly drooling
It's no life for you; stop all that screwing
You're packing your bags; you're coming with me"

The desire to rescue someone from abject poverty and self-inflicted abuse shows a want to assist in the aiding of someone who exists in a perpetual cycle of degeneration. While this aspect might be lost on some who lose themselves in the multiple time changes of the composition, it speaks to the band's desires in their formative years to escape from the area where they came from.

The first two installments in the saga of "Charlotte the Harlot" contain pathos and manage to generate sympathy for the main character and her plight while being descriptive about her deeds. The mythology takes a drastic turn of events in "Hooks in You" on *No Prayer for the Dying* and "From Here to Eternity" on *Fear of the Dark*.

The Number of the Beast

If there's an observation to be made about any artistic endeavor, it's that public perception tends to influence analysis. When it comes to any form of art that ties itself to the cloven-hoofed anti-hero, sometimes referred to as the Devil, there are those who possess an instant repulsion. It's only natural. Conditioning from organized religion over the centuries has made the adversary very real to some. Think back to Benjamin Christensen's *Haxan*, when the devil, played by the director in question, literally leaps out of a book and into reality.

To some, the Devil symbolizes evil, darkness, and temptation. To others, he's the ultimate symbol of rebellion and individuality. He's the angel who's well aware he can't defeat God and overthrow heaven, and he's bound to fall from grace, and yet, he draws a line in the sand and holds his ground against insurmountable odds. No matter what one's perspective on this being, there's bound to be a strong reaction to his likeness or the image, especially regarding the fabricated reality of art and popular culture.

For someone who views the spiritual realm as a very real place, "The Number of the Beast" might be a source of dread. For the occultist, the thought of Aleister Crowley's claims to being the great beast 666 might come to mind. It might appear to be a subject matter meant to enhance the song for the listener who ascribes to neither of the previously mentioned beliefs. So, where does "The Number of the Beast" fall into? Which category does the song belong to? Well, none of them. The song merely interprets a dream, which has much less to do with any occultist or esoteric belief and more with psychology.

And because it's impossible to mention this field without mentioning Sigmund Freud, it's his theories on dreams that we'll be consulting during this selection of the discourse. It was Freud's theory that dreams emanate from various factors, particularly experiences and organic stimulation from the physical world.

Freud equated dreams to operations conducted by the unconscious mind that had a variety of interpretations. These included wish fulfillment, desires, and motivations that our conscious mind tends to suppress. Freud's manifest and latent content theory can be seen in Steve Harris' lyrics. A dream's manifest and latent content implies what we remember upon waking up (manifest) and its hidden psychological meaning (latent.) The lyrics to "The Number of the Beast" involve a person's "mind staring back at them" and being placed in an existential state where the boundaries of reality and fantasy become intertwined.

"I left alone; my mind was blank
I needed time to think
To get the memories from my mind

What did I see? Can I believe it?
Was what I saw that night real and not just fantasy?
Just what I saw in my old dreams
Were they reflections of my warped mind staring back at me?
'Cause in my dreams, it's always there
The evil face that twists my mind and brings me to despair"

From the opening lines, the narrator makes it quite apparent that the story he's recounting is one where the lines between fantasy and reality are blurred and aren't as discernible in black and white as we'd like to think. This aspect is illustrated effectively in the music video, which uses footage from several classic horror films. These examples certainly do an exquisite job of illustrating the manufactured reality that exists within the realm of film. And, as anyone familiar with Federico Fellini understands, film is a medium that continually walks between the realms of the real and the fantastic.

"Torches blazed, and sacred chants were praised
As they start to cry, hands held to the sky
In the night, the fires are burning bright
The ritual has begun. Satan's work is done."

Now, these lyrics, which incorporate the details from the dream in a first-person narrative, can easily be taken out of context for anyone who, for the lack of a better term, wants to "clutch their pearls" at the aspect of a band promoting primitive superstitions regarding devil worship or satanism. (But that never happens, does it?) These lyrics deserve praise for framing a narrative of a dream in such vivid detail that it places the listener within a world where reality, much like art, becomes entirely subjective.

Run to the Hills

Both "Invaders" and "Run to the Hills" share common ground. They're both songs that chronicle different periods of history in which people are subjected to an invader's heel. They both spell out the plight and brutality of an armed conflict. However, "Run to the Hills" differs in both the expansiveness of the subject matter and the narrative style that shares the perspectives of both the invader and the subjugated.

While "Invaders" chronicles the clash between the Norsemen and Saxons, "Run to the Hills" transports its narrative across the Atlantic Ocean and a few centuries further in time to depict the cultural genocide of the Native Americans at the hands of the American settlers who were in search of fulfilling the "prophecy" of what's known as Manifest Destiny. That is, the belief that it was the sacred duty of America to expand its borders from coast to coast.

Remarkably, "Run to the Hills" doesn't simply retell the moments of battle to give the listener a glimpse of the conflict that Invaders does. Despite the song's big chorus, which makes it almost too perfect for commercial airplay, the structure of the lyrical content tells the story from both sides. It highlights both the injustices brought on by westward expansion and the xenophobic mindset of "taming the savages."

"White man came across the sea.
He brought us pain and misery.
He killed our tribes; he killed our creed
He took our game for his own need
We fought him hard; we fought him well
Out on the plains, we gave him hell
But many came, too much for Cree
Oh, will we ever be set free?"

Interestingly enough, the term "Cree" refers to the indigenous people who live in Canada. While the rest of the song is relatively ambiguous about the tribe being persecuted, utilizing the terms instantly identifies the geographic location. As the years have gone on, the cruel treatment from the Canadian and American governments towards their own indigenous people has persisted in one way or another. In this passage, you can see the frustration and hopelessness of the situation.

"Soldier blue in the barren wastes
Hunting and killing a game
Raping the women and wasting the men
The only good Indians are tame
Selling them whiskey and taking their gold

Enslaving the young and destroying the old"

The perspective from the cavalry (Soldier blue in a barren waste) is depicted in the middle and third verses of the song. Certainly, it makes no pretense of the outlook that has been shared by many regarding indigenous people. In fact, the lyric "the only good Indians are tame" is very similar to a quotation attributed to American general Phillip Sheridan, who remarked, "The only good Indian is a dead Indian." During the enslavement and resettling of the indigenous people to reservations, the addiction to alcoholism became rampant. Perhaps one of the most remarkable aspects of "Run to the Hills" is its subtext and the fact that it was written by a band who once existed in the realms of poverty and were themselves marginalized in the aspect of division in social class.

While there's very little to discuss regarding philosophy, "Run to the Hills" gives an objective look at history and examines a narrative from both sides, illuminating some of the injustices that have once existed and continue to be perpetrated on a large scale.

Gangland

At this point, Iron Maiden's lyrical content was moving away from the poverty-stricken alleyways of the East End, with the exception of "22 Acacia Avenue." "Gangland" takes us into the underbelly of an urban environment where crime rules the street. The criminal mind decides life and death, and, as the song so aptly puts it," dead men tell no tales."

The fascination with those who sit in judgment over their fellow human beings is both a source of fascination and repulsion. While we fear and despise these individuals for their callous actions, we also feel drawn to their complete disdain for the social morays and their gravitation toward various forms of transgression.

> "Shadows may hide you, but also may be your grave
> You're running today; maybe tomorrow, you'll be saved
> You pray for daylight to save you for a while
> You wonder if your children will face the killer's smile"

What I find most fascinating about the song's opening verse is that it transplants the listener into a world where murder is commonplace and injects one of the familiar tropes from gothic horror. "Praying for the daylight to save you for a while" instantly conjures up a small, isolated village in the shadow of Dracula's castle and the residents warning visitors that they shouldn't be caught outside when the sun goes down. Terror becomes universal in just a few lyrical passages. The juxtaposition of gothic folklore and crime that grips an inner city is remarkable storytelling that grabs the listener's attention.

> "Face at the window leers into your own

But it's only your reflection still; you tremble in your bones

How long can you hide? How long till they come?
A rat in a trap, but you've got to survive
Once you were glad to be free for a while
The air tasted good, and the world was your friend
Then came the day when the hard times began
Now you're alone but alive for how long?"

"Gangland" is a surprising departure, considering how many songs on the first two albums championed the outsider living on society's outer fringe. "Face at the window leers into your own. But it's only your reflection still; you tremble in your bones" is a stark depiction of how life on the edge results in the loss of humanity and a troubled existence where crime and transgression are not only the sole means of survival but also formulate a path towards self-destruction. What "Gangland" ultimately depicts is the life of crime that exists among those who live in poverty and how it's the only means of escape but also the ultimate downfall.

Hallowed Be Thy Name

Looking back through the pages of English history, a macabre fascination has always existed with capital punishment. One of the most notable was the Tyburn procession, where the condemned were paraded through the streets on a cart while draped in white sheets to the site of their execution. The morbid ceremony was a public event, gathering the number of spectators normally reserved for sporting events and pop concerts.

No other form of execution was more visceral than the punishment dealt to traitors, known as hanging, drawing, and quartering. After being hung, though not killed outright, the condemned were then emasculated, their bowels torn open and burned in front of them, and then mercifully beheaded. Meant to serve as a deterrent against treason, heads were usually placed on London Bridge.

A famous protest against public execution in London came in the form of an essay written by William Thackery entitled "Going to see a man hanged." The writer had witnessed the public execution of Francois Courvoisier, a French servant condemned for murdering his boss. Thackery described in detail the plight of the condemned man in his final moments as a black hood was draped over his head and a hangman's noose was tightened around his neck.

The final song on *The Number of the Beast* places the listener in the mind of a criminal as the final moments of his life play out, like some drama taking place on a public stage. Perhaps" Gangland's" placement on the album before this song is fitting, as "Hallowed be Thy Name" presents the inevitable conclusion to a life of crime.

Steve Harris' composition is another that seamlessly blends lyrical passages and music to create an atmosphere that takes the listener on a journey. "I'm waiting in my cold cell when the bell begins to chime…Reflecting on my past life, and it doesn't have much time. 'Cause at 5 o'clock, they take me to the Gallows Pole. The sands of time for me are running low." It's virtually impossible not to be completely swept away by the opening lyrical passage that paints a vivid picture of the condemned in their final hours.

The lyrical descriptions are highlighted by a melancholy atmosphere provided by the music. Then, out of nowhere, a sudden time signature shift jolts through the listener like a charge of electricity at the realization that reality has broken the calm. The final rites being read by the priest and a final look at the world through the bars of the cell initiate a sense of existential dread as it becomes apparent that life is fleeting.

> "Can it be that there's some sort of error?
> Hard to stop the surmounting terror
> Is it really the end, not some crazy dream?
> Somebody, please tell me that I'm dreaming
> It's not easy to stop from screaming
> The words escape me when I try to speak
> Tears flow, but why am I crying?
> After all, I'm not afraid of dying
> Don't I believe that there never is an end?"

The lyrics of "As the guards march me out to the courtyard. Somebody cries from a cell, "God be with you " If there's a God, why has he let me go?" resonates deeply as it establishes the theme explored within the song in the concluding passages. From a moment where the existence of an omnipotent being is introduced to the aspect of the condemned realizing that his existence will carry on after departing from the physical world.

> "When you know that your time is close at hand
> Maybe then you'll begin to understand
> Life down here is just a strange illusion"

"Hallowed be Thy Name" is remarkable in that it allows us to gauge the human experience and offer a perspective of someone who has to come to terms with their own mortality and the possibility of what lies ahead. Similar to *The Wall* by Jean-Paul Satre, the condemned are given a voice to express their inner feelings about the situation that they find themselves in. The crime for which the narrator is charged, and the execution are absent from the narrative entirely. It's simply the human experience that the song focuses on, and in doing so, Harris offers an in-depth look at a subject matter that we can all relate to.

The World Is Theirs…

The Number of the Beast shows a band reaching outside of the East End. Not just in terms of popularity and success but in subject matter that had the probability to address a wider range of topics and situations. The following year would see a massive shift in the musical landscape where the disciples of Iron Maiden would introduce a new phenomenon known as

Thrash Metal to the masses. Iron Maiden was also about to transcend into a new era that would see a notable change in the band's lineup and their capabilities soar to new heights.

Piece of Mind (1983): An Exploration into New Frontiers

"...every man is a unique autonomous center of individual consciousness, energy, and will—a soul, in a word. Like a star shining and existing by its own inward light..."

-Israel Regardie, *The Tree of Life, An Illustrated Study in Magic*

If we consider the personnel of Iron Maiden as representatives of different elements that are essential for the completion of a ritual, in this case, an album of collected musical works, then the constant line-up changes on their albums up to this point might have forced the group to splinter off in a mass of directions that resulted in a proverbial mishmash.

For any other band, this might have been the case. But Steve Harris, the magician at the altar, would have never allowed such events to transpire. The shift about to occur would be one of stability that would carry the group off for the rest of the decade. Clive Burr, who had been behind the kit since the debut album, would be the next musician to depart. His replacement would be the swashbuckling and raucous Nicko McBrain. With a new lineup in place, McBrain would have a tall order to fill as the group began work on their fourth studio full-length, *Piece of Mind.*

The clever play on words was all part and parcel to the tongue-in-cheek nature that the group possessed behind the scenes. The illustration from Derek Riggs that adorned the album's cover made a lasting impression on anyone who saw it. Eddie is depicted in the confines of a padded cell. Three chains attached to his neck and the evidence of a lobotomy made it clear that this was a new direction for the band. The journey the group had taken out of the East End was fully realized. On the next several albums, Eddie's design would take on various forms that would each be utilized to establish the aesthetics of each album.

Listening to the first four albums in succession, *Number of the Beast* might be viewed as a transitory stop on a spiritual journey. Comparable to the title character in Alejandro Jodorowsky's film, *El Topo,* Iron Maiden had assumed the role of the black-clad gunslinger, crossing a wasteland and discovering something about themselves that they may have not been aware of before. Lyrical content would encompass a broad spectrum of items that would include literature ("Quest for Fire," "To Tame a Land"), philosophy ("Sun and Steel," "Die With Your Boots On"), film ("Where Eagles Dare"), history ("The Trooper"), occultism ("Revelations," "Still Life") and even in the case of "Flight of Icarus," mythologies that had been passed down for thousands of years.

Piece of Mind was much more than an album; it was a literal Odyssey in which Iron Maiden probed into worlds both seen and unseen and took their listeners with them.

Where Eagles Dare

You only get one chance to make a first impression, and the opening moments on any album can be the most critical. When it came to Nicko McBrain making an impression on anyone listening to *Piece of Mind* for the first time, he succeeded at the beginning of "Where Eagles Dare." Nicko's thundering drum roll generates excitement and awe. It matches the high-velocity twin guitar assault of Adrian Smith and Dave Murray, which catapults the listener into the fray of conflict.

"Where Eagles Dare," based on the movie of the same name, is a pummeling shock to the senses and manages to capture the daring commando raid that took place in the film. As a song, it serves as a showcase for Nicko's remarkable talent that's on full display, just as the rest of the album will. The film's story of a Nazi base being raided by Clint Eastwood and Richard Burton is certainly action-packed. As the subject material for a song, it's one of the best ways to articulate the driving force of the band's ambition at this point in their career.

"Where Eagles Dare" carries on the tradition that was established on *Killers* and *Number of the Beast* a high-velocity opener that immensity shakes the listener and establishes a template for what's going to follow. Like the daring commando raid in the film, this can be interpreted as a statement of intent on the part of the band themselves as they strive to go into brave new worlds that only the truly daring would travel to. Appropriating film and other art forms to relay a personal statement is certainly nothing new, and one can easily deduce that the lyrical content reinforces this and provides a visual companion to the music's driving force.

"It's snowing outside
The rumbling sound of engines roar in the night
The mission is near
The confident men are waiting to drop from the sky

The blizzard goes on
But still they must fly
No one should go
Where eagles dare

Bavarian Alps that lay all around
They seem to stare from below
The enemy lines a long time passed
Are lying deep in the snow"

The template established on "Where Eagles Dare" illustrates the boldness and tenacity of Iron Maiden's direction, a realm to which only the daring travel. If the purpose of ritual is to manipulate reality, this is where everything truly begins to take shape. The forces had been conjured, the stage was set, and now this new era of Iron Maiden was officially underway.

Revelations

At the start of this chapter, I discussed how introducing new members into the fold can make a notable difference in how the material takes shape. Had it not been for the introduction of Bruce Dickinson, the realms of spiritualism and metaphysics might not have been so vividly developed. Revelations sees Dickinson laying the groundwork for what would be on subsequent Iron Maiden releases and the solo career that he would embark upon following his departure after the release of *Fear of the Dark*. "Revelations" combine multiple elements from occultism and weave them together to create a narrative of awakening and enlightenment.

The mark of any good artist is the willingness to circumvent trends and common practices. As Orson Welles once remarked, there's a necessity to being "out of step" with the times. The satanic imagery that the band had utilized on *Number of the Beast* had perplexed some of the public. "Revelations" might have elicited a similar response from those who heard "After Forever" by Black Sabbath after hearing their earlier material. Named for the final book in the Bible, "Revelations" has less to do with Christian imagery and more with Bruce Dickinson taking the listener on a spiritual odyssey. The opening verse, taken from an old English hymn, is a cry for mercy and a longing to commune with a higher power.

> "Oh, God of Earth and Altar
> Bow down and hear our cry

Our earthly rulers falter
Our people drift and die
The walls of gold entomb us
The swords of scorn divide
Take not thy thunder from us
Take away our pride"

The passage indicates the failing of the human race, between the corruption of government (Our earthly rulers falter), the greed and ambition of humanity (the walls of gold entomb us), and the onslaught brought on by hatred and war (the swords of scorn divide.) The concluding lines can almost be seen as a plea for spiritual healing and removing hubris and apathy. This is the importance of any philosophical thinking, not just the interpretation of meaning, but how it can apply to society several hundreds of years later.

"Just a babe in a black abyss
No reason for a place like this
The walls are cold, and souls cry out in pain
An easy way for the blind to go
A clever path for the fools who know
The secret of the Hanged Man, the smile on his lips"

The description of being a babe in a black abyss can possibly allude to Aleister Crowley's terminology of the path of a magician. Known as being a "babe of the abyss." Some might refer to this as a crossroads, the moment where the magician ultimately chooses to divorce himself from the physical world and sacrifice ego for a higher communion, or one who chooses to follow self-interest. "An easy way for the blind to go" alludes to the left-hand path that the spiritually bankrupt and materialistic tread down.

This passage describing the fool on the clever path and the secret of the "hanged man" relates to the Tarot, and considering how the song contains several allusions to the doctrines of Thelema, it can be assumed that this passage relates to the *Book of Thoth*, which itself relates to the Thoth tarot deck designed by Crowley.

The fool in many tarot decks represents the continuing journey of the human experience. Like Joff from Ingmar Bergman's *The Seventh Sea*l, the Fool represents the journeyman, wandering, growing, and evolving. The juxtaposition of the Hanged Man in the lyrical passage indicates the two paths that the fool can embark upon. When the card comes into play during a reading, it represents wisdom, intuition, and spiritual growth. Reversed, it represents materialism and selfishness. Revelations, while normally associated with the Bible, instead take a form that alludes to the "revealing" of the truth in the unseen world.

The concluding lyrics of "Revelations," "It is you," are remarkably simple yet contain considerable meaning. The paths we take in life are similar to that of the magician. This can be attributed to the Hermetic axiom of "as above, so below," where our actions are reflected in unseen worlds. The magician who chooses how to apply his craft for the greater good or reasons fueled by his self-interest isn't so different from our choices. This duality of right or wrong, good or evil, above and below, is a critical aspect of the human experience, and the choices we make and the paths we follow determine the outcome of our destinies.

Flight of Icarus

We go from spirituality and search for esoteric knowledge to the rich pantheon of myths and legends created by the Ancient Greeks. The saga of Icarus is one of hubris and certainly ushers in the warning of the importance of following the rules and the advice of our elders.

The myth is the story of Icarus and his father, Daedalus, who escape captivity with the aid of wings attached to their bodies with wax. Despite the warnings not to fly too close to the sun, Icarus cannot resist the allure and falls to his death when the wings melt off. We often use this myth in our own discourse regarding taking on too much and straying off the path we intend to follow, usually with the phrase "flying too close to the sun."

"Flight of Icarus" represents one of the most important aspects of any mythology or form of folklore, and that's the ability to retell it in various ways. This is something that we've seen in films such as *Titus* and *Throne of Blood,* where two of Shakespeare's most notable plays, *Titus Andronicus* and *Macbeth,* are retold in new settings that allow them to be enjoyed by a broader audience. Julie Taymor's ability to construct a world that has no definitive time period and Akira Kurosawa's repurposing of *Macbeth* to the world of feudal Japan ensures that these stories possess longevity. The way in which Iron Maiden does it is nothing short of remarkable and a testament to the band's consistent ability to build new worlds and expand upon the existing ones.

> "As the sun breaks, above the ground
> An old man stands on the hill
> As the ground warms, to the first rays of light
> A birdsong shatters the still"

The mental image created in the listener's mind allows the classic myth to take on a whole new life as it's retold for an entirely new audience. The pulsing rhythms accompanying the lyrical content create an atmosphere that retells the saga of the boy who decided to fly too close to the sun. Even the lyrical passage "Now his wings turn to ashes, to ashes his grave" illustrates the classic myth in a new and thought-provoking way that perfectly coincides with the atmosphere of the musical arrangement.

Perhaps what makes this retelling even more interesting is that while Iron Maiden are theoretically retelling the tale, they also refuse to follow the mythology as a self-fulfilling prophecy. Iron Maiden were on their way to dominating the decade, and not once would they ever be in danger of flying too close to the sun.

Die With Your Boots On

"Men of the South, it's better to die on your feet than live on your knees."

-Emiliano Zapata

One of the biggest factors that make *Piece of Mind* such a unique album is just how much depth it contains in relation to its lyrical content and how far it separates itself from the past endeavors that the band had accomplished. The purpose of philosophy and the pursuit of enlightenment all come down to the theories of evolution. The will to power and the necessity for personal growth.

"Die With Your Boots On" might seem like another typical metal anthem of personal expression and individuality, but there's much more to the lyrical content. While there's certainly a fair amount of gusto and self-determination within the song's lyrics, it also deals with independence and separation from the confines of organized religion, the empty promises of politicians, and the importance of forging one's own path.

"Yeah, another prophet of disaster
Who says this ship is lost?
Another prophet of disaster
Leaving you to count the cost
Taunting us with visions
Afflicting us with fear
Predicting war for millions

In the hope that one appears"

The aspect of the prophet standing on the mountain and espousing visions of the end of the world is certainly nothing new. From Nostradamus to Jim Jones to Heaven's Gate, the masses are always willing to listen to those who moan about fear and uncertainty regarding the future of the human race. It's the near-perfect example of "meet the new boss, same as the old boss." This is further reflected in the lyrical passage, "No point asking when it is. No point asking who's to go. No point asking what's the game. No point asking who's to blame."

"In 13, the beast is rising
The Frenchman did surmise
Through earthquakes and starvation
The warlord will arise
Terror, death, destruction
Pour from the eastern sands
But the truth of all predictions
Is always in your hands"

The "13" that the lyrics describe is the thirteenth book of Revelations and continues the album's theme of spiritualism in various forms. The 13th chapter vividly describes that beast rising from the sea with seven heads, and the question of whether or not war can be waged against it is posed. Remarkably, this chapter played an important part in "The Number of the Beast," as the concluding passage reads, "Let the person who has insight calculate the number of the beast, for it is the number of a man. That number is 666."

The 13th chapter in Revelations was also used by author William Conrad Golding in *Lord of the Flies*, with one of the main characters discussing that the beast is not a mythological reality but the inherent wickedness in man. "Die With Your Boots On" is remarkable as it talks about the fear generated through prophets and Biblical text and makes the case that the prevention of an apocalypse is in our hands. This separation of folklore and reality and divorcing ourselves from primitive superstitions to stand our ground in hopes of a better future is my personal interpretation of the song in question. The words of Zapata are alive and well in the song and remind us that it's better to die standing up than to live a lengthy existence in the throngs of servitude.

The Trooper

"Cannon to right of them,
Cannon to left of them,
Cannon in front of them
Volleyed and thundered;
Stormed at with shot and shell,
Boldly they rode and well,
Into the jaws of Death,
Into the mouth of hell
Rode the six hundred."

- Alfred Lord Tennyson, "The Charge of the Light Brigade."

If "Flight of Icarus" is a retelling of an ancient myth, then "The Trooper" can best be described as preserving the historical lineage of the United Kingdom. While there's little in metaphysics that can be deduced from "The Trooper," it vividly paints the saga regarding one of the most tragic blunders in military history. During the Crimean War, faulty military intelligence resulted in a British cavalry unit charging a battery of Russian artillery, later immortalized by Tennyson in his poem, "Charge of the Light Brigade."

Remarkably, as someone who does admire history a great deal, I find it fascinating that the charge of the light brigade is sometimes discussed with a romanticism. Yet, the same can't be said for Florence Nightingale's efforts in advancing the role of medical attention to wounded personnel during an armed conflict. Going to the well as it were, Harris' composition shows the developing ability to blend lyrical content with an atmospheric musical composition to place the listener into the fray as we charge headlong into the valley of death.

The galloping rhythm of "The Trooper" is again a place for Nicko McBrain to show off his skill and the new level of musicianship he's bringing into the fold. Harris' lyrical passages continually paint the imagery of battle and spell out the situation's futility for the British cavalry.

"The horse he sweats with fear. We break to run
The mighty roar of the Russian guns
And as we race towards the human wall
The screams of pain as my comrades fall
We hurdle bodies that lay on the ground
And the Russians fire another round
We get so near, yet so far away
We won't live to fight another day"

Through the music, we can hear the brigade galloping, witness the ill-fated charge as it occurs, and share the perspective of the 600 as they plummet toward their charge of folly. While not everyone might be familiar with the works of Tennyson and Sir Walter Scott, Harris' composition serves as a living history lesson, which certainly speaks to the talents and capabilities of Iron Maiden as a force of nature.

Still Life

Metaphysics and other practices involving seeking esoteric knowledge are often misconstrued as evil. Many notable occultists have pointed out that magic is neither good nor evil, as the user's intention defines its nature.

The concept that a band whose material contains complexity and lyrical content that's meant to be thought-provoking and insightful would somehow be involved in something such as satanism or primitive devil worship is certainly comical to our modern sensibilities. Needless to say, the accusations were made, especially in an era where "Satanic Panic" was a very real moral hysteria perpetuated by the more conservative elements of the establishment.

There is no better way to answer the false accusations of one's detractors than by expressing it through artistic outputs, with a bit of a satirical smirk thrown in for good measure. The smirk I refer to comes from what occurs before the song begins. A reverse message by Nicko McBrain informs the listener, "Do not meddle in things you do not understand." The message can be read in a variety of different interpretations. Still, the fact that it exists as a form of "backmasking" is one of the best uses of social satire, especially when one considers the ridiculous amount of accusations regarding messages of a similar nature from other bands.

A few years later, Judas Priest would be involved in a civil lawsuit that claimed that a subliminal message of "do it" existed on their album, *Stained Class*, and had mesmerized two youths, James Vance and Ray Belknap to form a suicide pact. The band was dismissed of all charges, and the case remains a point of contention for many as a lesson in the dangers of undiagnosed mental health.

To provide a discourse on "Still Life" in a metaphysical sense, we first need to delve into the song's title and the primary theme behind its structure. "Still Life," a common expression in the art world, describes an arrangement of objects in a painting. These usually consist of flowers, food, and sometimes animals.

If we take a moment to apply this to the magician, we can consider the altar of objects from which he practices his craft.

The altar, with its various implements arranged in a specific order to conduct a ritual to alter reality. Because many still life paintings contain inanimate objects, we can certainly assume that the ritual taking place in the song is bringing about a considerable change. Throughout the course of "Still Life," allusions are made regarding a pool of water. Water is one of the most significant elements not only in magic, but philosophy as well. Water is considered the giver of life, an essential part of the human body, and the sea has often been written about at great lengths as a forgiving and romantic location.

As one of the four base elements in ritual and ceremonial magic, water is a cornerstone for any practicing magician. In "Still Life," it takes the form of the reflecting pool, a location where the magician passes into nature and an unseen world guarded by the high priestess of the tarot deck. Some believe this is where the magician taps into their inner self, granting a better perception to those seeking it.

> "Take a look in the pool, and what do you see?
> In the dark depths there faces beckoning me
> Can't you see them? It's plain for all to see
> They were there. Oh, I know you don't believe me."

The opening verse establishes the magician becoming aware of the unseen world, and the skepticism met with the discovery from the uninitiated. Something "plain for all to see" certainly speaks to the willful ignorance of those who fail to look deeply at the world in which they exist. Another possible interpretation can allude to madness and delusion. Much like the babe of the abyss, there are two very real paths to consider, "Still Life" is subjective in how it presents its lyrical content.

"Oh, I've never felt so strange.
But I'm not going insane.
I've no doubt that you think I'm off of my head
You don't say, but it's in your eyes instead"

Sanity and the knowledge of what's unseen are both entirely subjective. One of the prevailing aspects of "Still Life" is that reality isn't as clearly defined as we would like it to be. The listener is left to interpret whether the magician has been given second sight or is merely a victim of his own delusions. "Hours I spend out just gazing into that pool. Something draws me there, but I don't know what to do." Perhaps the veil of the high priestess is being lifted. Perhaps the delusion brought about by insanity and madness has completely taken over.

"Now it's clear, and I know what I have to do
I must take you down there to look at them, too
Hand in hand then we'll jump right into the pool
Can't you see, not just me, they want you too"

The song's narrator continually speaks of nightmares. Once again, these can be interpreted as either visions from the world that lie beyond our grasp or the psychosis of dementia. It's unclear whether the Narrator wishes to take the skeptic to the other side of the veil or envelop them in the same madness they have begun to embrace. Nicko McBrain's back masked warning of "not meddling in things you don't understand" becomes more than a satirical smirk when "Still Life" arrives at its inevitable conclusion. "We'll drown together; it will be forever" implies there's no turning back once a particular path has been chosen. Madness and sanity, self-interest and enlightenment, both paths have their own unique outcomes. "Still Life" allows the listener to arrive at their own personal interpretation of the lyrics, allowing them to choose their own path.

Quest for Fire

The era of early man is certainly a source of fascination for anthropologists and those curious about species' origins. Gaining widespread interest in the subject is sometimes difficult, as while the histories of other ancient civilizations have their own mythologies, customs, and tales of conquest and innovation, prehistory is sometimes accompanied by misconceptions. For instance, Neanderthal Man was once thought of as a dim-witted brute, simply based on the fact that some of the earliest skeletal remains found belonged to one who had suffered from crippling arthritis. First published in 1911 and made into a full-length feature film in 1981, *Quest for Fire* is the saga of primitive man to obtain the source of light and heat, which is essential for survival.

> "In a time when dinosaurs walked the earth
> When the land was swamp, and caves were home
> In an age when prize possession was fire
> To search for landscapes, men would roam
> Then, the tribes they came to steal their fire
> And the wolves they howled into the night
> As they fought a vicious, angry battle
> To save the power of warmth and light"

The source material that "Quest for Fire" is based upon is certainly relevant in 1983. The book, which chronicles the odyssey of a tribe looking for fire to ensure their survival, exists in a truly unique world. Many of the descriptions within the song lyrics are in line with the original text, written by J.H. Rosney, such as the "cannibal tribes and beasts." The book features many intricate tribes, forged alliances between men and animals, and the growing implication of technological advancement. These were crucial in 1911, as Europe was still in the throes of the Industrial Revolution, and a clockwork of alliances would plunge the continent into the First World War in 1914. The Cold War, with its arms race and tensions between NATO and the Warsaw Pact countries, was just as volatile, and the struggle to obtain power was something on the minds of many nations.

"So, they plowed through the forest and swamps of danger

And they fought the cannibal tribes and beasts

In the search to find another fire

To regain the power of light and heat"

"Quest for Fire" takes the listener on a journey to the dawn of history. More than once, I've described the music of Iron Maiden as ritualistic, as it shifts the paradigms of reality. Within our own imaginations, we trek across the harsh landscapes and navigate the many dangers that present themselves to the characters within the song.

Sun and Steel

One of the greatest attributes of philosophical thought is that something formulated and pinned hundreds and thousands of years ago can be applied to our lives in various ways. Secluded from the West for hundreds of years, Feudal Japan was a land completely absorbed within itself, with its laws and traditions within the island nation. Bushido is among the many traditions romanticized through various mediums, particularly the films of Akira Kurosawa. The code adhered to by the Samurai has captivated generations of those who have chosen to live by the sword.

"Sun and Steel," a composition by Bruce Dickinson and Adrian Smith, takes us away from the metaphysical and culture associated with England and transports us to Feudal Japan and one of its most notable figures, Miyamoto Musashi. A swordsman and philosopher, he's considered by some to be one of the greatest swordsmen who ever lived. He developed a philosophical method of swordsmanship and authored a text known as *The Book of the Five Rings*. "Sun and Steel," embraces the philosophy of Musashi and relays it to a wider audience.

"The way of the warrior, you took it as your rite" is a direct reference to Bushido, the code the samurai lives by. Bushido, known as the way of the warrior, was not just an integral part of the Samurai but a practice that still permeates many aspects of modern Japanese society.

> "Through earth and water, fire and wind
> You came at last; nothing was the end
> I'll make a cut by fire and stones
> Take you and your blade, break you both in two
> Break you both in two"

Musashi's *The Book of Five Rings* represents each chapter by a base element: Earth, Air, Fire, Water, and Void. Similar to the four elements used in Western occultism, and the fifth, spirit, when all four are represented by the magician. Void, the fifth book by Musashi, isn't mentioned in Dickinson's lyrics, and perhaps this isn't by accident, as spirit is only present when the other four elements are also represented. Void, a chapter that contains Musashi's philosophical perspective, becomes represented in the song itself which contains a fair amount of duality in the lyrical passages.

> "Sunlight, falling on your steel.
> Death in life is your ideal.
> Life is like a wheel."

Sun and steel, which can possibly allude to the relationship between nature and combat, are further represented by the wheel, which symbolizes the never-ending cycle of life that continues uninterrupted. "Life is like a wheel and it's rolling still," the concluding lyrical passage in the song, all too perfectly sums up the persistence of time. Aside from the philosophical content that Bruce Dickinson brought into his several lyrical compositions, "Sun and Steel" is where the vocalist introduces his love of swordplay, which will become essential to many of his notable contributions over time.

To Tame a Land

There's no denying that *Piece of Mind* sees Iron Maiden undertaking a journey into realms left unexplored in previous releases and seen an incredible amount of development in terms of world-building. These attributes are certainly present in the album's final song, "To Tame a Land." Remarkably, it is one of the most interesting and brilliant adaptations of the source material to ever be completed.

The history of Frank Herbert's science fiction epic, *Dune,* has had an interesting relationship with its adaptations. Alejandro Jodorowsky, the visionary behind *El Topo* and *The Holy Mountain,* attempted an ambitious undertaking that would have seen a cast that included David Carradine, Mick Jagger, Orson Welles, Salvadore Dali, and have music supplied by Pink Floyd and artistic elements from H.R. Geiger. Described by some as the mother of all unmade movies, we're left to speculate what might have been. The adaptation that did make it to the screen was brought to us by another groundbreaking visionary, David Lynch. And while the aspect of the same individual who crafted *Eraserhead* taking on a world that's beyond fantastic might have been good on paper, the end result has often been mocked and ridiculed by cinephiles and fans of the book.

"To Tame a Land" takes Herbert's vision and applies it to the song. Like so much of the material on *Piece of Mind,* Harris demonstrates his ability to manufacture a reality within his compositions and place the listener into an environment almost as an out-of-body experience. Even if someone were completely unfamiliar with the source material, "To Tame a Land" utilizes atmospheric feeling and descriptive lyrical passages to take us to a distant planet far away from our own.

> "He is the King of all the land
> In the Kingdom of the sands
> Of a time tomorrow
> He rules the sandworms and the Freemen

In the land amongst the stars
Of an age tomorrow"

The opening lyrical passage places the listener in a setting that conjures up images of a far-off planet where the sand dunes span for what appears to be an eternity. "Sandworms and Freemen" certainly establishes beasts that defy anything that we may be used to and a world where masses are subjugated under the rule of a monarch.

"Body water is your life.
And without it, you would die.
On the desert, the planet Dune
Without a stillsuit you would fry
On the sands so hot and dry
In a world called Arrakis
It is a land that's rich in spice
The sand riders and the mice
That they call the 'Muad' Dib.'"

While it's apparent that the song takes place in a world unlike ours, there is something to be said regarding the names Herbert uses to describe the locations and people in his world. While they're certainly part of a larger mythos, they're close enough to our language that they could be Middle Eastern or Mediterranean. This sense of familiarity allows the listener's imagination to wander and create a reality within their own mind.

What I truly find awe-inspiring about "To Tame a Land" is the same aspect that I noticed with "Flight of Icarus:" the capability to adapt source material and present it to a larger audience who might not have been familiar with it.

A Piece of Mind Goes a Long Way

To say that *Piece of Mind* was a landmark achievement for Iron Maiden would certainly be a considerable understatement. Not only have they settled on a lineup that would greatly increase their upward trajectory in both popularity and complexity for the rest of the decade. They have thoroughly left the East End of London far behind them. While there's no denying that their formative years had allowed them to hone their craft and probe the aspects of poverty and urban blight, there was a whole world waiting for them, both in terms of conquest and exploration.

Adding Bruce Dickinson up front and their continued collaborations with Martin Birch opened several new realities to formulate and manufacture. *Piece of Mind* established Iron Maiden as a force that could tackle subjects other bands still shied away from. With the arrival of thrash metal and bands like Metallica and Slayer increasing ferocity and angst, Iron Maiden took a different route with the continued exploration of subjects such as philosophy, folklore, and history.

From the magician's perspective at the altar, the veil of the high priestess was now thoroughly stripped away. The secrets of King Solomon's temple were now firmly in their grasp. The physical locations that had been a considerable part of Iron Maiden's growth were now behind them, and subsequent releases would take their listeners on a journey that no one could have foreseen.

Powerslave (1984): The Duality of Life and Death & Ongoing Saga of the Ancient Mariner

Piece of Mind had certainly ushered in a new era for Iron Maiden. A solid lineup was cemented in place that would define their forward progression for the rest of the decade, and the lyrical themes and concepts that the band was now embracing were far and away more complex than they had been on prior releases. Accompanying these new topics were more intricate musical arrangements that illustrated a massive shift in development.

1984 is a unique year for many reasons, as many events on the world stage continue to play a major role in our lives today. From the rising death toll of people affected with AIDS to the multiple events that were shifting the paradigm of world politics and the introduction of the Macintosh computer, the physical world was drastically changing. As for the manufactured reality formulated by art, music, literature, and film, one work alone is synonymous with the year in question, and that's George Orwell's novel of the same name. For those who thought the dire predictions of dystopia in the novel might come true, it was certainly starting to feel that way.

As for Iron Maiden, the dystopian predictions and growing emphasis on technological advancements would undoubtedly be integral to their next album, *Powerslave*. An ambitious undertaking that would highlight Bruce Dickinson's songwriting talents, new worlds were ready to be explored. While many of *Piece of Mind*'s facets would be carried over, *Powerslave* would see the band reach new operatic heights of technical mastery.

At the core of *Powerslave* exists the philosophical concept of duality. Opposites such as life and death, the Hermetic axiom of as above and below, and other topics are thoroughly examined together as if the entire album is a thesis in its own right. From the concepts of war ("Aces High" & "Two Minutes to Midnight") to the skill of the combatant ("Flash of the Blade" & "The Duelists".) *Powerslave* would be a remarkable moment. Looking at it from the magician's perspective, this is where theory and practice are documented and presented to a neophyte.

An indication of how ambitious *Powerslave* was can be exhibited on the album's artwork. Artist Derek Riggs formulated a design that accentuated the front and back of the album and brought Ancient Egypt to life. The front, which featured a grandiose temple with Eddie's face adorning a statue of a pharaoh and a funeral procession marching up the steps to enter, displays the reverence the Ancient Egyptians had for their god-kings. A duality of life and death is first seen on the back of the album, as we see a sarcophagus within the temple, the pharaoh's final resting place. The duality that Riggs' artwork presents illustrates the reverence from the living and the cold reality of mortality. This will be explored on the album's title track.

Aces High

"We shall go on to the end; we shall fight in France, we shall fight on the seas and oceans, we shall fight with growing confidence and growing strength in the air, we shall defend our Island, whatever the cost may be, we shall fight on the beaches, we shall fight on the landing grounds, we shall fight in the fields and in the streets, we shall fight in the hills; we shall never surrender..."

-Sir Winston Churchill

As they previously did on *Number of the Beast* and *Piece of Mind,* Iron Maiden spares no moment to establish a template on *Powerslave* that grips the audience in a complete frenzy. Like "Invaders," the tenacity of armed conflict and aggression is vividly illustrated, and like "Where Eagles Dare," Steve Harris once again examines the mammoth struggle of the Second World War. "Aces High" follows this template, and its lyrical content and accompanying music serve as the perfect opener for an album of such magnitude.

"Aces High" depicts the "Battle of Britain." Following the German invasion of Poland and the subsequent fall of

France during the Second World War, it appeared that England might be next to capitulate to Adolf Hitler's war machine.

The contest between the German Luftwaffe and Royal Air Force that took place over the skies of England would determine the balance of power in the years to come. The dog fights that took place between Spitfires and Mescherschmidts became legendary. The carnage that rained down from the sky in the form of several air raids, referred to as "the blitz," would only galvanize the British public and the steadfast determination of Prime Minister Winston Churchill. Described by the Prime Minister as "their finest hour," Churchill's words, "Never in the field of human conflict have so many owed so much to so few," praised the brave men of the R.A.F.

The mid-paced opening of "Aces High" erupts into a frenzy and disturbs the calm that existed just a few moments prior. The opening lyrics that follow place the listener into a frantic situation. In another example of the world-building that Iron Maiden had mastered at this point in their career, we're thrown headlong into a battle between the two air forces and their contest for superiority over the skies.

"There goes the siren that warns of the air raid
There comes the sound of the guns sending flak
Out for the scramble, we've got to get airborne
Gotta get up for the coming attack
Jump in the cockpit and start up the engines
Remove all the wheel blocks. There's no time to waste
Gathering speed as we head down the runway

Gotta get airborne before it's too late"

The lyrical content vividly describes the epic struggle within the heat of battle. From a philosophical standpoint, "Aces High" can be viewed as the determination and focus of Iron Maiden as a cohesive unit. The rush of the Spitfires to take on the challenge of the Luftwaffe can be viewed as the continuous path forward that Iron Maiden was following. There's no denying that "Aces High" establishes a tone that will ebb and flow as the rest of the album unfolds.

Presentation is critical with any art form. The following year, when Iron Maiden released their *Live After Death* album, recorded during the band's "World Slavery" tour, "Aces High" isn't just the opening song; Churchill's speech serves as the introduction. This provides context for the subject material that "Aces High" is based on and elicits the same emotional response that the R.A.F. had when they went into battle. The combination of Churchill proclaiming "We will never surrender" immediately followed by the opening salvo of the song grips the listener and puts them in the cockpit as they journey into the fray.

2 Minutes to Midnight

"I'm fed up to the ears with old men dreaming up wars for young men to die in."

-George McGovern

We oil the jaws of the war machine
And feed it with our babies"

The "napalm screams" and a "prime-time Belsen feast" articulate the carnage and destruction that get brought out on the evening news. Napalm bombing strikes, which had been a common practice during the American war in Vietnam, was one of the first major conflicts that were broadcast to the world on a large scale and led to the public's discontent with the war overseas. The aspect of a "primetime Belsen feast" is something that not only emphasizes media coverage of global conflict but also calls back to one of the darkest chapters in the history of humanity, the Holocaust.

Bergen Belsen, a Nazi Concentration Camp, was liberated by the Royal Army. Newsreel footage was on site to capture the inhumane conditions of the camp and the captured SS guards being tasked with burying the bodies. The footage shocked the world to its core. It depicted an aspect of carnage that no one wanted to believe existed. "2 Minutes to Midnight" calls back on the events and displays them in such a way that reminds us that the inhumanity of the human race continues to persist.

"Oiling the jaws of the war machine" and "feeding it with our babies" recounts the old anti-war sentiment of old men sending young men to die for them in their wars. The concept of babies being thrown into some sausage grinder illustrates the unwilling sacrifice of the young and the commodification of others to serve.

"As the mad men play on words
And make us all dance to their song
To the tune of starving millions
To make a better kind of gun"

"Making us all dance to their song" can be interpreted differently. The first is the aspect of politicians and world leaders controlling the populace's destinies, much like marionettes, with the "tune of starving millions" comparable to the pied piper of Hamelin leading the rats and children away.

Another interpretation that can be made is something that calls back to the "Danse Macabre," a depiction of the living and the dead dancing with one another. Known as the "dance of death," a title Iron Maiden would use for one of their later albums, the illustration was prominent in the Middle Ages and served as part of the conclusion for Ingmar Bergman's *The Seventh Seal*, a film that depicted the existential dread regarding death and the afterlife.

"2 Minutes to Midnight" is the ultimate depiction of what author Barbara Tuchman might have described as the "March of Folly." The entire composition depicts the sensationalism and profitability of war and the fate of the world being guided by the hands of corruption and power. It's a grim indictment of the human race.

If there was any doubt as to the bleak nature of the song and its subject matter, the accompanying music video, which was one of the best achievements for the band up to that point, left no pretense as to its apocalyptic nature. Like many early music videos that contained mostly performance footage, the effort put forth in "2 Minutes to Midnight" crafted a narrative within the video that further illustrated the cloak-and-dagger aspect of warfare. Two mysterious corporations, one symbolized by a ram's head and the other by the Eye of Horus, are locked in a struggle.

These symbols are another example of duality that exists throughout the duration of *Powerslave*. The Ram's head, often associated with Aries's astrological sign, corresponds to Mars, the God of war in Roman mythology. The Eye of Horus, which was used in Ancient Egypt during the Old Kingdom, was used as a symbol of protection and well-being; these polar opposites engaged in conflict with one another illustrate that warfare is indeed never-ending and has existed in a persistent state from the days of ancient civilizations to the present.

Much of the video surrounds a group of mercenaries preparing for a mission. This aspect of "hired guns" being used to carry out the wishes of those who pull the strings brings many of the lyrical concepts presented in the song to life. The ending of the video, which shows the screen going blank with the audible sound of machine gun fire, leaves us to ponder what the future holds for us as those who wield power remain in control.

Losfer Words (Big 'Orra)

There's something to be said about being an artist and taking your work seriously while also not minding some self-depreciation at your own expense from time to time. "Losfer Words (Big 'Orra)" joins "Transylvania," "The Ides of March," and "Genghis Khan" as an instrumental track that delivers power and prominence.

However, there is a unique aspect that makes it the most unique out of all of them. "Transylvania" had that gothic atmosphere that was commonly associated with Hammer films, whereas "The Ides of March" gave a hint to the calm before the storm, and "Genghis Khan" certainly captured the ferocity of a galloping horde, "Losfer Words (Big 'Orra)" has a tongue-in-cheek bit of humor that adds to its' charm. Playing on how a cockney accent might pronounce the term "Loss for Words (Big Horror)," it shows the group's ability to laugh at their own expense.

Even the title seems to hint at not having lyrics written and the horror and dread of writer's block. Either way, it's a great way of showing that even the most serious artists and practitioners of their craft can have a laugh at themselves from time to time. Just look at Lou Reed's performance in *Get Crazy* to see this aspect fully realized.

Flash of the Blade

"I see you stand like greyhounds in the slips,

Straining upon the start. The game's afoot:
Follow your spirit; and upon this charge,
Cry 'God for Harry! England! and Saint George!"
-William Skahepear, Henry V, Act III, Scene I

On *Piece of Mind,* Bruce Dickinson introduced new concepts to be explored. Among these is the saga of the swordsman. "Sun and Steel" brilliantly depicted that there was much more to swordsmanship than knowing how to use one. Indeed, there is a philosophy attributed to the craft. The dedication to achieving skill, poise, and technique are all part and parcel of any discipline, whether it's the search for esoteric knowledge, honing your skills as a musician, or gaining a fundamental understanding of existence.

"As a young boy chasing dragons
With your wooden sword so mighty
You're St. George or you're David and you always killed the beast
Times change very quickly and you had to grow up early
A house in smoking ruins and the bodies at your feet"

The opening passage recounts the fantasy of childhood, where we learn a fundamental aspect of artistry and one possessed by the magician, the manipulation of reality. One can easily see a young child and his wooden sword, losing himself in his own imagination, slaying dragons and storming castle walls in a display of unabashed showmanship. "You're St. George or you're David and you always killed the beast" refers to an important part of English Lore.

In looking through art history, there's a good chance you'll come across various paintings depicting St. George, the patron saint of England. St. George, who, according to legend, slaughtered a dragon demanding tribute from a village, is often depicted as doing so.

There's most likely a historical fact behind this legend, much like St. Patrick driving the "snakes" out of Ireland. This allegory most likely alludes to Christianity becoming the dominant religion and driving away the pagan beliefs of the Celtic tribes. The saga of St. George killing the dragon most likely represents a revolt against an oppressive ruler. Still, the many depictions of St. George battling a dragon resulted from many artists being inspired by the legend.

"The smell of resigned leather, the steely iron mask
As you cut and thrust and parried at the fencing master's call
He taught you all he ever knew, to fear no mortal man
And now you'll wreak your vengeance in the screams of evil man"

The journey is always much more exciting and sometimes more important than the destination. From childhood fantasy to learning the craft at the hands of a master, Dickinson's lyrics place the listener behind the fencing mask and into the close quarters of combat. The lyrical passage " You'll die as if you lived in a flash of the blade" certainly reinforces the concept of obsession and passion being an all-encompassing one that students of fencing and the endless pursuit of knowledge devote their energy to.

The Duelists

The concept of two songs following one another with varying takes on a similar subject matter is present in "The Duelists." Like the placement of "Aces High" and "2 Minutes to Midnight," which examine warfare as both a necessary evil for self-preservation and the commodification and profiteering done by those in control, "Flash of the Blade" and "Duelists" embody two different aspects of the same concept. While "Flash of the Blade" depicts the discipline and poise it takes for a swordsman to hone his craft, "The Duelists" chronicles the swordsman's application of these lessons. This is a fundamental part of any discipline, known as theory and practice.

> "He threw down a glove. You made the mistake
> Of picking it up, now you're gone
> The choosing of guns or fighting with swords
> The choice of weapons is done
> He'll tear you apart, as soon as you start
> You know you don't have a chance"

The expression "throwing down the gauntlet" is synonymous with issuing a challenge. This dates back to the aspect of challenging someone to a duel. The opening verse certainly illustrates the aspect of egoism, where the individual knows he will certainly falter, but sacrifices logic in favor of emotion. These aspects of duality, which have to do with the human brain, are where bad decisions are made; in this case, it's salvaging honor and reputation over being thought of by others as a coward.

"Ready to start, the duel begins.
The best man wins in the end
A lunge and a feint, a parry too late
A cut to the chest and you're down
Seeing the stain, then feeling the pain
Feeling the sweat on your brow"

The duality between the two people in close-quarter combat, adversaries fighting against one another, is vividly placed within the listener's imagination. The accompanying music certainly simulates the illusion of sword and flesh piercing one another, and the lyrical content vividly depicts the concept of one realizing that death is imminent.

"A cut and a thrust, a parry, a blow
A stab to the heart and you're down
The Angel of Death hears your last breath
Meanwhile, the Reaper looks on"

The aspect of the reaper being near calls back to "2 Minutes to Midnight" and the Danse Macabre of life and death being intermingled with one another, once again, duality playing an integral role throughout the duration of *Powerslave*. "The Duelists" perfectly illustrates the swordsman and his application of theory into practice and the struggle between logic and emotion within the human mind.

Back in the Village

When it comes to any art form that exists as a manufactured reality, the lasting cultural impact that it can make on its audience is truly remarkable. On *Number of the Beast*, the impact of the BBC program *The Prisoner* on Bruce Dickinson is certainly apparent in the song of the same name. "Back in the Village," a song whose title references a prominent location of the television series, takes us back into the world where one desires not to be a number but a free man.

> "Turn the spotlights on the people
> Switch the dial and eat the worm
> Take your chances, kill the engine
> Drop your bombs and let it burn
> White flags shot to ribbons
> The truce is black and burned
> Shellshock in the kitchen
> Tables overturned"

An aspect of "Back in the Village" that makes it one of the more unique offerings on the album is its ambiguity and vague descriptions that can be applied to different scenarios, whether or not anyone is familiar with the television series. The opening verse can easily describe an air raid and the apathy in a state of warfare. White flags, a sign of surrender being shot to ribbons, illustrate the desire to offer no quarter to a potential peace offering. The vivid depictions of tables overturned in a depiction of absolute carnage can even be attributed to the visions of war as depicted by Pablo Picasso in his famous painting, Guernica.

> "Throwing dice now, rolling loaded
> I see sixes all the way
> In a black hole and I'm spinning
> As my wings get shot away
> Questions are a burden
> And answers are a prison for oneself
> Shellshock in the kitchen
> Tables start to burn
> Back in the village again, in the village
> I'm back in the village again"

The references to *The Prisoner,* such as number 6 and always being back in the village no matter how hard the chief protagonist attempts to escape, are recognizable to anyone familiar with the television show, as are the allusions to questions being a burden and answers being a self-contained prison. For the sake of argument, let's assume that we're analyzing the song from the point of view of complete objectivity and divorcing any preconceptions that the song relates to the television program. We're met with both a concept of existential dread and a continual state of warfare and suffering.

"No breaks on the inside
Paper cats and burning barns
There's a fox among the chickens
And a killer in the hounds"

Further divorcing ourselves from the show and ignoring the fact that these lyrics refer to Number 6 being hunted whenever he attempts to escape and ends up back in the village, we can make note of the "fox among the chickens" and the "killer in the hounds" as ways to describe the animalistic nature that exists in warfare and that these beasts are always on the hunt. Indeed, we will always find ourselves back in the village, where warfare and torment are never-ending, as we have no hope of escaping the confinement of a world where hope is nonexistent.

Powerslave

Throughout human history, there have been attempts to explain and understand mortality and the existential crisis of not knowing what awaits us as the final curtain falls. While there are many interpretations and beliefs, very few have had a major impact on the Western world than those of the Ancient Egyptians, particularly those from *The Book of the Dead. The Book of the Dead* can easily be seen as the precursor to many Western beliefs that espouse a period of judgment that culminates in a joyous afterlife or eternal damnation.

One of the most complex religious texts ever written, *The Book of the Dead* chronicles the journey from death to the afterlife. Anubis weighs the heart of the deceased against the feather of Maat, the Egyptian goddess who represents order, balance, and justice. The journey into the afterlife would begin if the heart is lighter than the feather. However, if the heart outweighed the feather of Maat, Ammit, described as the "eater of the soul," would devour the wicked, thus ensuring damnation.

One of the primary aspects of this belief system is the myth of Osiris. Osiris, the god-king of Egypt, ruled the land with his wife, Isis. According to the myth, Osiris' brother Set, fueled with rage and contempt, murdered Osiris to usurp the throne and dismembered him, casting his remains into the Nile. To conceive their child, Horus, Isis resurrected Osiris, who becomes lord of the underworld.

This mythology was tied directly to every succeeding pharaoh who came to rule Ancient Egypt, with the god-king equating to Horus while he was on earth and Osiris when he crossed over into the afterlife.

Powerslave, the album's title track, offers the perspective of the recently deceased. We have a philosophical discourse on the trappings of belief, no matter what they might be. In an age where monarchy appears to be an archaic system of government and the principle of a god-king seems ridiculous, *Powerslave* brings us into mythology and theology and dissects them both.

When I was living this lie, fear was my game
People would worship and fall
Drop to their knees
So, bring me the blood and red wine
For the one to succeed me
For he is a man and a god
And he will die, too"

The lyrical passage of the Pharaoh recognizes that the worship of his subjects was brought about through fear and paranoia. When he realizes that the whole aspect of godhood is a fabrication, he wishes the same fate to befall his successor. Aside from dissecting the belief system that the Pharaoh once ruled under, one can find a political commentary within these lyrical passages. "Fear was my game" is an aspect that many dictatorships and oppressive governments have utilized throughout history to make their subjects fall in line.

"Now I am cold, but a ghost lives in my veins
Silent the terror that reigned

Marbled in stone
A shell of a man God preserved
For a thousand ages
But open the gates of my hell
I'll strike from the grave"

The curse of the mummy is firmly ingrained into popular culture as a viable threat. This concept might never have entered our consciousness without Howard Carter's opening of King Tutankhamun's tomb. For many years, an unsubstantiated rumor existed that a curse was inscribed in the tomb that read, "Death will come swiftly for those who enter my tomb." Years later, modern archaeologists have debunked this.

The curse was dreamt to sensationalize a string of deaths that occurred following the tomb's discovery. It was later discovered that bacterial spores might have contributed to some of these. The aspect of an Egyptian curse has been largely dismissed as a myth. However, it has certainly persisted throughout film, literature, and music as a consistent source of entertainment.

The premise of being a "slave to the power of death" is itself a self-fulfilling prophecy. Death is the certainty that unites all individuals, regardless of social status or position. The existential dread that looms from not knowing what lies beyond the final curtain has persisted since the dawn of time. *Powerslave* is one of many that remind us that the physical realm and what exists after our eventual passing are two very different aspects.

The Rime of the Ancient Mariner

"An orphan's curse would drag to hell
A spirit from on high;
But oh! more horrible than that
Is the curse in a dead man's eye!
Seven days, seven nights, I saw that curse,
And yet I could not die."

-Samuel Tayler Coleridge, "The Rime of the Ancient Mariner"

There's something about the sea that has inspired generations of writers, artists, and musicians. One of the four principal elements the magician utilizes as conceptualized by Aristotle, the sea encapsulates a sense of awe and fascination. The wonders it's inspired, from sea monsters to the legendary lost city of Atlantis, have resonated with us for centuries and will most likely continue to do so.

Of all the tales woven about the ocean and its many mysteries, there is perhaps none more grandiose than The Rime of the Ancient Mariner, written by Samuel Taylor Coleridge and published in 1798. To fully grasp the impact of how a poem such as this would have the impact on the imagination it did, we must first consider the time period. England, at the height of its ambitions of a global empire, relied on its navy for exploration and importing goods, conquest, and defense.

The history of the Royal Navy is full of tales that almost seem otherworldly in how spectacular they are. There is the saga of the doomed Franklin Expedition, trapped in the ice while searching for the northwest passage. Sir Francis Drake overcoming the might and power of the Spanish Armada. There is the famous mutiny on the HMS Bounty and the Battle of Trafalgar, where Horatio Nelson defeated the navies of Napoleon Bonaparte, and himself became a martyr after being felled by a French sharpshooter.

Coleridge's poems can be compared to *The Monk* by Matthew Lewis, as they deal with familiar aspects of our reality and integrate fantastical elements that stir deep within our imagination. *The Rime of the Ancient Mariner* tells the story of a man being stopped on his way to a wedding, where a mariner tells him about a voyage he undertook several years prior. The story involves a ship stuck in the ice until an albatross guides them to safety. After killing the albatross, the ship ends up in peril, and the albatross is hung around his neck like a crucifix. One by one, the ship's crew dies, and the Mariner goes into great detail about looking into their eyes and facial expressions. Naturally, this is most likely where the expression "albatross around my neck" in describing a heavy burden comes from. The Mariner is doomed to recount his tale for the rest of his life, himself serving as a cautionary tale.

Like *The Monk,* in which a pious clergyman named Ambrosio succumbs to temptation and makes a pact with the devil, there's a semblance of morality that Coleridge's poem instills in its listeners. Most notably with the mariner learning to respect all creatures.

To take an epic poem of such magnitude and rely on it as source material for a song might have been a daunting task for anyone, and the final song on *Powerslave* is much more than a mere song; it's an operatic magnum opus. Weaving complex musical arrangements, excerpts from Coleridge's poem, and a lyrical re-telling of the tale, very few songs come close to the reality that Iron Maiden created with "Rime of the Ancient Mariner." Like the magician at the altar who weaves all elements together to impact the world they live in, Iron Maiden takes us on a journey that defies all limits of perception.

> "Hear the rime of the ancient mariner
> See his eye as he stops one of three
> Mesmerizes one of the wedding guests
> Stay here and listen to the nightmares of the sea"

The choice of the opening lyrics was appropriate and fitting. Like the mariner himself, the listener is told to "stay here and listen" to the tale and "hear" the story that's about to be told, and like the wedding guest, we, too, will become mesmerized.

> "Driven south to the land of the snow and ice
> To a place where nobody's been
> Through the snow fog flies on the albatross

Hailed in God's name, hoping good luck it brings
And the ship sails on, back to the North
Through the fog and ice and the albatross follows on"

The progression of the song and the lyrical passages serve as a journey onward as the listener becomes completely enveloped in the mariner's tale. "Driven South" and "Back to the North" articulate the journey of the ship, and the multiple time changes of the song rock back and forth as the wind fills the sails; we can almost smell the salt air as the ship departs the frigid arctic waters and heads to a warmer climate. We're then introduced to the catalyst that will transport us to a place of dread and death.

"The mariner kills the bird of good omen
His shipmates cry against what he's done
But when the fog clears, they justify him
And make themselves a part of the crime"

While killing the albatross certainly catalyzes what occurs afterward, it also provides a glimpse into human nature. The crew's shock and repulsion over the unprovoked action are quickly dismissed when there's no immediate repercussion against them. It displays the lack of empathy that we sometimes have when situations don't impact us directly. However, things soon turn for the worse, for the lack of a better term.

"The albatross begins with its vengeance.

A terrible curse, a thirst has begun
His shipmates blame bad luck on the mariner
About his neck the dead bird is hung"

Imagine the fear and dread of being at sea, far away from civilization, and the only resources for nourishment and hydration being the supplies that were packed on board during departure. Harris' lyrics incite dread by simply mentioning, "A thirst has begun." The paranoia and mass hysteria in the run-of-events give birth to the mariner carrying his own burden in the form of a literal albatross around his neck.

One of the two passages that Harris includes from Coleridge's original poem takes place during a slow atmospheric interlude within the song. A narrative voice creates the illusion that the mariner is speaking to us directly. The accompanying music and sounds of the creaking shipboards elicit a sense of dread as the curse is described and the crew, aside from the mariner, meet their ghastly fate.

"One after one by the star-dogged moon
Too quick for groan or sigh
Each turned his face with a ghastly pang
And cursed me with his eye
Four times 50 living men
(And I heard nor sigh nor groan)
With heavy thump, a lifeless lump
They dropped down, one by one."
-Samuel Taylor Coleridge, "The Rime of the Ancient Mariner"

Then, as if the ship passes from its place of dead reckoning, Dickinson's voice is heard as he recounts the aftermath of the situation's torment:

"The curse it lives on in their eyes
The mariner he wished he'd die
Along with the sea creatures
But they lived on, and so did he.

And by the light of the moon
He prays for their beauty, not doom
With heart, he blesses them
God's creatures, all of them too

Then, the spell starts to break.
The albatross falls from his neck
Sinks down like lead into the sea
Then, down in falls comes the rain"

Much like a Greek tragedy, *The Rime of the Ancient Mariner* begins and ends in the same place, with the mariner recounting his tale to the wedding guest. "The mariner's bound to tell of his story.

To tell this tale wherever he goes" implies the aspect of eternal recurrence, as described by Nietzsche, of certain events reoccurring in an infinite loop. *Rime of the Ancient Mariner* possesses some of these theories, such as humanity always having to atone for consequences for disturbing nature and the aspect of stories needing to be retold to ensure their longevity so we can continue to learn from them.

Rime of the Ancient Mariner can be seen as a near-perfect example of oral tradition. By applying a stylized retelling of Coleridge's poem, its longevity was ensured, and the tale of the mariner will be told for many years to come. The mariner was bound to tell his story, and thanks to the genius and application of one, Steve Harris, it appears that it always will.

Powerslave was a landmark achievement for Iron Maiden. The realms in which they had begun to explore were rapidly increasing. As a critic who attempts to apply the Socratic method in everything, all aspects of the world around us should be seen as subjective and open to discourse and interpretation. This would continue on subsequent releases.

To Be Continued in *Metaphysics of The Beast Vol 2.*

ALSO, FROM ST ROOSTER BOOKS

From Tim Murr

The Gray Man

978-1799252177

Motel on Fire; Stories

978-1543039016

Neon Sabbath; Stories

978-1721039708

My Skull is Full of Black Smoke: Stories

979-8680276099

Thirsty and Miserable: A Critical Analysis of the Music of Black Flag

979-8609363220

Texas is the Reason: Five Decades of the Texas Chainsaw Massacre

979-8374744392

Summer's Venomous Kiss

979-8378167012

Whatever Happened to Spiderbaby Jane? b/w Snake Eater

979-8860069916

Collection/Various Authors

To Be One with You: An Anthology of Parasitic Horror 2018 featuring Paul Kane, Marie O'Regan, Jeffery X Martin, Peter Oliver Wonder, Adam Millard, DJ Tyrer, David W Barbee, Ross Peterson

978-1724516787

Kids of the Black Hole; A Punksploitation Anthology featuring Sarah Miner, Chris Hallock, Paul Lubaczewski, and Jeremy Lowe

978-1072962724

The Blind Dead Ride Out of Hell; A Literary Tribute to the Amando de Ossorio Films featuring Sam Richard, Heather

Drain, Paul Lubaczewski, Mark Zirbel, Jeremy Lowe, and Jerome Reuter

979-8692365187

A New Life by Paul Lubaczewski

979-8615384066

Blood & Mud by John Baltisberger

The God Provides by Thomas R Clark

979-8520227076

3 Hits from the Holler by Paul Lubaczewski

979-8707581984

Abhorrent Siren by John Baltisberger

978-1955745024

Let the World Drown: An Anthology of Sea Horror featuring Brian M Sammons, Lee Franklin, Jedediah Smith, AK McCarthy, Anthony S Buoni, BE Goose, Paul Lubaczewski, Jeremy Lowe, John Baltisberger, and Carter Johnson

979-8739852915

Souls in a Blender by Lamont A Turner

979-8494735201

Hungry Cosmos by Reed Alexander

979-8776862472

Black Friday: An Elder's Keep Collection by Jeffery X Martin

978-1955745093

Abhorrent Faith by John Baltisberger

978-1955745093

Short Stories About You by Jeffery X Martin

9798438145318

I Never Eat...Cheesesteak by Paul Lubaczewski

979-8440821415

Hunting Witches by Jeffery X Martin

979-8832793955

Saint's Blood by Ryan C Bradley

979-8804031863

As the Night Devours Us by Villimey Mist

979-8834327097

Parham's Field by Jeffery X Martin

SummerHome by Thomas R Clark

979-8838185136

The Ridge by Jeffery X Martin

979-8354516568

Through the Mist and the Madness: An Analytical Thesis on the First Three Metallica Albums by Jerome Reuter

979-8354143696

Like a Ton of Bricks by Paul Lubaczewski

979-8367912081

The Flock by Jeffery X Martin

979-8365780941

A Prayer from the Dead by Thomas R Clark

979-8393890742

Wax Figures by Aaron Weese

979-8390704202

Razor Blade in the Fun-Size Candy: A Horror Comedy Anthology edited by Paul Lubaczewski featuring Jeff Strand, John Wayne Communale, Bridgette Nelson, Robert Essig, Tony Evans, John Baltisberger, Mikki Nelson-Hicks, RJ Bennetti, Christine Morgan, Damien Casey, Kyra R Torres, Kenzie Jennings, Michael Allen Rose, Nikolas P Robinson

979-8395371195

Bleeding Out in the Rain by Lamont A Turner

979-8852235145

Brooklyn Hardcore by Eddie MacNamara

979-8850638979

Even More Monsters by Paul Kane

979-8859240890

Electric Funeral: Black Sabbath and the Cultural Landscape 1970-1975 by Jerome Reuter

979-8854150477

Droplets: Stories by Paul Lubaczewski

9798879721935

Under a Starless Sky by Lamont A Turner

979-8324229252

www.ingramcontent.com/pod-product-compliance
Ingram Content Group UK Ltd.
Pitfield, Milton Keynes, MK11 3LW, UK
UKHW040947240325
456642UK00001B/14

9 798330 316342